# INSIGHT COMPACT GUIDE

# BELFAST
## & SURROUNDINGS

*Compact Guide: Belfast* is the ultimate quick-reference guide to Northern Ireland's dynamic capital. It tells you everything you need to know about its attractions, from the fine Victorian architecture to the intimate alleyways and pubs, from the fascinating museums to a shipbuilding legacy that included the *Titanic*.

This is one of more than 100 titles in Insight Guides' series of pocket-sized, easy-to-use guidebooks edited for the independent-minded traveller. Compact Guides are in essence travel encyclopedias in miniature, designed to be comprehensive yet portable, as well as up-to-date and authoritative.

## Star Attractions

An instant reference to some of Belfast's top attractions to help you set your priorities.

*Linen Hall Library p15*

*St Malachy's Church p18*

*Grand Opera House p22*

*Crown Liquor Saloon p22*

*Botanic Gardens p28*

*Ulster Museum p28*

*Shipyard heritage p35*

*City Hall p38*

*Belfast Castle p47*

*River walks p52*

*Excursions p58*

# BelFast

## Introduction

Belfast – Titanic Town ...................................................................5
Historical Highlights...................................................................10

## Places

**Route 1:** The Linen Town...............................................................**15**
**Route 2:** Dreaming Spires .............................................................**25**
**Route 3:** Titanic Town ..................................................................**30**
**Route 4:** North, to the Poorhouse ...............................................**37**
**Route 5:** Napoleon's Nose ...........................................................**46**
**Route 6:** Troubled Times .............................................................**48**
**Riverside Walks**.............................................................................**52**
**Excursions:**
       **1:** Gold Coast, Viking Lough......................................**53**
       **2:** St Patrick's Country................................................**55**
       **3:** A Georgian Flowery Vale ......................................**57**
       **4:** In the Steps of a Giant ...........................................**58**

## Culture

Architectural Heritage...................................................................**61**
Art as History, Art as Mural...........................................................**62**
Literary Lives...............................................................................**63**
Festivals ......................................................................................**65**

## Leisure

Drink and Food ...........................................................................**67**
Nightlife ......................................................................................**70**
Shopping .....................................................................................**71**

## Practical Information

Getting There ...............................................................................**73**
Getting Around ............................................................................**74**
Facts for the Visitor......................................................................**75**
Belfast for Children......................................................................**77**
Accommodation...........................................................................**78**

Index ...........................................................................................**80**

# Belfast – Titanic Town

Without its baggage of troubles, and the resultant 30 years of media coverage which sent its flames around the globe, Belfast could have been seen in another light: as an extravagance of pubs and churches; as a seaport rich in Victorian buildings on the western edge of Europe where they built the ill-fated *Titanic*, as the home of Irish linen; as host to Nobel Laureate poet Seamus Heaney's campus, George Best's schooldays, Van Morrison's streets, and a liquor saloon preserved as a national monument immortalised in *Odd Man Out*, Carol Reed's seminal film noir.

But who knew of it before *les événements* of 1968? Its Unionist government dissociated itself from all that was marketable to visitors as being in any way Irish. Its tourist literature listed which minor British royal opened which public building but gave scant mention of the abundant '*craic*', of the in-your-face northern humour, of pubs pulsing with music, of Guinness downed in the Crown Liquor Saloon with the cockles and mussels that have been gathered with relish from the surrounding sea loughs since Mesolithic peoples settled here 8,000 years ago.

*The Harbour Office today*

*Peace mural*

But then the IRA hijacked the Civil Rights movement of 1968, creating in counter-blast the Protestant paramilitaries, and from the 1970s to the 1990s if you mentioned the city anywhere in the world, locals associated the word 'Belfast' with car bombs and rioting. Today, however, the climate has changed: you can stroll fearlessly past fashionable chain stores, looking up at portraits of Victorian heroes carved on the facades of the one time linen merchants' warehouses built to the style of Italian *palazzi*.

## Location and climate

Belfast sits in a saucer of hills in the northeast of Ireland, at the head of a broad sea lough at the mouth of the River Lagan, which flows east into the Irish Sea. It is the capital of the six counties of Northern Ireland, an integral part of the United Kingdom of Great Britain and Northern Ireland. On a clear day, from the lough's mouth, you can see Scotland 30km (20 miles) to the east. Dublin, capital of the 26-county Republic of Ireland, lies 160km (100 miles) to the south.

At 67m (217ft) above sea level, the city lies 54°39N, 6°13W, as far north as Canada's Labrador and Denmark's Copenhagen, and as far west as Land's End and the Isle of Skye. So the Gulf Stream delivers a daytime average of 18°C (65°F) in the sunniest months of June, July and August, with 6 hours of sunshine. Occasionally in July, temperatures reach 30°C (low 80s°F), but on summer nights the thermometer drops to 11°C (50°F) and winter

5

minimum temperatures average 2°C (36°F). April and May are the driest months, with 2in (50mm) each of the year's rainfall of 33in (84cm). But you can meet all the seasons in one day, so pack your mac and a sweater, whatever the month. Up-to-date information is available from Weathercall (tel: 0891 500427) or Marinecall (tel: 0891 505365).

## Population

In the 1951 census 30.4 percent declared themselves Presbyterian, 29.7 percent Church of Ireland (Anglican/Episcopalian), 25.9 percent Catholics, 7.8 percent Methodists and 1.5 percent Protestants/other. Jews numbered 1,140, Moslems 44, Hindus 17, Sikhs 14. Few people registered zero affiliation. When civil rights marches began in the late-1960s, 98 percent of a Falls ward declared itself Catholic, with 84 percent reading the Nationalist *Irish News*. Nearby, in the 99 percent Protestant Shankill, 3 percent took that paper (for the racing); their loyalty was to the Unionist *Belfast News Letter*. Two decades later, even after ghetto to ghetto pogroms had laid waste whole streets, intelligence maps showed the same divisions.

*Playtime in Ormeau Park*

6

According to 1998 figures, Belfast's inner city has 300,000 citizens, a slight recovery from an exodus of 25 percent over the previous two decades. The population of the greater Belfast area is 476,000.

## Old history

Wave after wave of cultures sailed up Belfast Lough, raiding, trading, intermarrying. The Celts landed 7,000 years after the Neolithic hunter-gatherers, ushering in the Iron Age. No-one is sure about the Romans' involvement, if any, but St Patrick's landfall was in AD432, 50km (30 miles) southeast. Two centuries later comes the first mention of Belfast when the Celts noted their predecessors, the Cruithin and Uliad, battling at Béal Feirste, 'the

*Civic Festival participants*

approach to the sandbank ford', on the River Lagan. By 900, Vikings were dragging their boats over the sandbank.

*The Vikings came in force*

Across this same sandbank in 1177 came John de Courcy, with his mailed and mounted Anglo-Normans. He annexed Ulster against the wish of his monarch, Henry II, who knew that John would become its sovereign in all but title. But de Courcy never subdued the chieftains. Celt and Norman intermarried, forming a new land-owning Catholic class, the Old English. Over centuries, they, the Celtic Irish, the Dissenter Planter Scots, fought: sometimes for the Crown, sometimes against. Peasants reared crops and children, watching both fall in battle.

A Scot, Edward the Bruce, was first up the lough in 1315, to be crowned king and die in battle. From then on, Belfast's English garrisoned castle was destroyed, rebuilt, demolished, retaken. England's Elizabeth I, knowing Ireland would side with Catholic Spain, needed to lay waste the Catholic chieftains. Her first attack on Belfast was easily repulsed in 1571 by O'Neills holding this wooded, impenetrable, Gaelic-speaking valley in their fiefdom. But in 1573 her favourite, the Earl of Essex, beat them, quartering survivors during his victory banquet, but failing to build a lasting town. The place fell, in 1603, to an even more ruthless criminal adventurer, Sir Arthur Chichester.

*Elizabeth I*

So it was Chichester who created Belfast, populating it in 1606 with Scots Dissenter tradesmen, some of whose descendants 30 years later set sail for the Americas conscious that, although the Catholic Irish were at the bottom of the privilege ladder, they themselves were no more than second-class citizens. Protestants (established church), Dissenters (Presbyterian) and Catholics were the divisions that persisted through another 200 years of skirmish, and set the demographic patterns for recent troubles.

Chichester's followers sided with the Crown in the English Civil War but Belfast fell in 1648 to a superior Scots army on Parliament's side. The town's leaders made another mistake, welcoming the accession of James II – but they changed their mind when he insisted on Catholic burgesses. James seized the town in 1689, but the Protestant William of Orange soon regained it. A US consulate was established in Belfast in 1796 and, fired by the spirit of the American and French Revolutions, Belfast's Dissenter middle class led the doomed 1798 rebellion, designed to free the entire island from British rule. But French troops, on whom they counted, never made it north.

*King Billy*

Sectarianism took root. Even after the Act of Union in 1800 dissolved Ireland's Parliament and created the United Kingdom of Great Britain and Ireland, a literate Catholic artisan class challenged its Protestant neighbours.

The American War of Independence ruined the linen trade in outlying districts, and Catholic weavers combined as Defenders. Protestants countered with the Peep o' Day Boys and formed the Orange Order in 1795. And so, entrenched, Catholics and Protestants battled for centuries for their slice of an inadequate economic cake.

## Modern history

World War I (1914–18) saved Ireland from imminent civil war. Thousands of armed militants on both sides joined up and the city prospered in the war effort. Dublin's Easter Rising of 1916 failed, but the Anglo-Irish War of 1919–21 led to a treaty setting up the Irish Free State. However, Protestant resistance in the northeast meant that six counties, to be called Northern Ireland, remained part of Britain.

While the terms of the treaty led to civil war in the new Free State, Unionists in the North had got what they wanted. Belfast, Northern Ireland's capital, became the seat of, in the words of its first prime minister, 'a Protestant parliament for a Protestant people'. For half a century, religious discrimination in education and employment was endemic. High unemployment never became an election issue, however. But education was, and is, segregated by religion. The Protestants' bogeyman was an Ireland dominated by the Catholic church; the Catholics' *bête noire* was a Unionist government led by a minor squirearchy.

And so it might have continued, with occasional bouts of sectarian violence, had not the 1947 Education Act delivered university education on merit, not privilege. The non-sectarian university-based Civil Rights Movement marched in accord with the spirit of 1968 which swept American and French campuses. Then, after the head-in-the-sand government brutally suppressed the marchers in full view of the world's media, a moribund IRA hijacked equality's cause, provoking Protestant counterparts.

It took 30 years, the abolition of the local parliament, the imposition of direct rule from Westminster, the creation of a Dublin–London political axis, major population shifts and the loss of 3,000 lives before the province voted in 1998 for peace through a power-sharing Assembly.

## The industrial heritage

French (Protestant) Huguenots fleeing persecution brought linen to the banks of the River Lagan, but it was still a cottage industry when Presbyterians, ushering in the Industrial Revolution, imported power-driven cotton machinery in 1771. Soon the population was 27,832, the majority employed in mills. Protestant spinners were well paid, Catholic weavers not. Trade was volatile, firms ruthless, unions illegal, unemployment high, housing intolerable, typhus and cholera inevitable, strikes and protests frequent. Facing quality competition, Irish cotton was in trouble by the 1830s. But economic revival came with the in-

*Stormont Castle, built to house Northern Ireland's parliament*

*Linen has a long tradition*

dustrialisation of linen, the railway age, and port improvements. By 1856 Mulholland's linen works was the world's largest. When the 1864 American Civil War cut off cotton supplies, linen boomed, bringing prosperity for owners and a 15-hour day for workers.

In 1853 Edward Harland, who trained under George Stephenson of *Rocket* fame, hired Belfast's skilled labour, at low wages, to build iron not wooden ships. By the 1870s Harland & Wolff was the world's largest shipbuilder, linked to the White Star Line, which shipped emigrants to America. Their *Oceanic* broke transatlantic records, but the *Titanic* sank on its maiden voyage. A spin-off, Belfast Ropeworks, became a world leader. Gallaher's Tobacco, Irish Distillers, plus tea and ventilation plants followed. Belfast had become Ireland's only industrial city.

*Still in business: Harland & Wolff*

## A tale of two men

Neither planners nor bombers were kind to Belfast. In the 1960s a lacklustre provincial civil service failed to recognise the unique vernacular environment that the architect Charles Lanyon had created a century before.

Lanyon had seized the day when the Chichesters, who had run the town as their private fiefdom for two and a half centuries, went broke. The profligate 4th Earl's debts were such that he was imprisoned before he was 21 and a more prudent 5th Earl sold off the city to speculators. Lanyon, although himself a bounder, had a vision that made the city what it is (*see page 61*). But this meant nothing to sullen 1960s planners, and great buildings were demolished, replaced by flaking concrete. The bombers had a go at much that was left, leaving a city rich in unplanned parking lots with a few score of fine buildings standing out.

## Peace and town planning

With the first inklings of peace, hide-bound planners swept flyovers through inner-city villages, and Belfast rekindled its affection for its potent Victorian and scant Georgian heritage. Laganside Corporation has rediscovered Lagan's banks and captured a public imagination fired by Victor Robinson's keynote Waterfront Hall and plans for a cobbled Cathedral cultural quarter. Entrepreneurs, previously dulled by a mendicant economy, have seized their moment. From the City Hall south to the University, streets are packed with café-bars and disco-pubs.

Employment in the service industries rises and those in peace and reconciliation counselling prosper. At the start of the 21st century, the city stands on the cusp. Will the new-found engagement with good design prosper? Or will profit crowd it out, just as Robinson's beautiful Hall has been overshadowed by multi-storeys? Belfast's residents and visitors should keep their fingers crossed.

# Historical Highlights

**7,000BC** The Ice Age retreats. Mesolithic peoples gather cockles from River Lagan mudbanks.

**3,000BC** Neolithic peoples build Giant's Ring dolmen near Belfast.

**500BC** Celts name this place Béal Feirste, Belfast, 'approach to the sandbank ford'.

**AD432** St Patrick lands at Saul.

**666** Belfast's first mention in history books: a battle at the ford between Cruithin and Uliad.

**c900** Viking marauders work shallow-draught ships up the Lagan.

**1014** Brian Ború, High King of Ireland, defeats the Vikings.

**1177** Celtic foot soldiers stand little chance against the horsemen of Anglo-Norman adventurer John de Courcy, who fords the river at Belfast against Henry II's express instruction.

**1315** Scot Edward the Bruce invades with 6,000 men to be crowned king and die in battle.

**1523** The Fitzgeralds 'brake a castell called Belfast' in 1523 as they did in 1512 and 1503, as did O'Donnells in 1489 and O'Neills in 1476.

**1571** O'Neill repulses Queen Elizabeth I's attack on Belfast, the first attempt at the bloody colonisation of Catholic Ulster, the most Gaelic and impenetrable of Ireland's four provinces and a possible ally to Spain's maritime ambition.

**1573** The Earl of Essex is gifted Belfast, routing the O'Neills at the ford and building a fort.

**1597** Shane O'Neill takes the English in Belfast Castle, slitting throats and disembowelling.

**1603** Sir Arthur Chichester is granted 'castle of Bealfaste' and founds a prosperous settlement.

**1606** Protestant Lowland Scots settlers are imported, bringing their trades and industry.

**1607** Ireland's princes flee the north, to Spain.

**1613** Belfast's charter of incorporation places it in the fortunes of the Chichesters for 200 years.

**1636** Alienated Presbyterian Dissenters sail for America. Storms force them back.

**1641** The citizens erect a rampart against attack by Irish and Old English rebels.

**1648** Belfast, loyal to the Crown, falls to Scots siding with Parliament in the English Civil War.

**1649** Cromwell takes Belfast by siege. The city is retaken by the Royalists in 1660.

**1685** The Protestant Corporation's welcome to Catholic James II is short-lived. James takes the undefended city in 1689, but William III's forces regain it in August that year.

**1690** William of Orange arrives, then marches south to defeat James at the Battle of the Boyne.

**1708** Belfast Castle is gutted by fire.

**1756** The first food riots occur.

**1757** 5th Earl of Donegall leases off Belfast. Protests as developers charge exorbitant rents.

**1760** The French capture Carrickfergus.

**1773** John Wesley describes the plight of Belfast's destitutes. Poorhouse planned.

**1776** St Anne's Church is completed.

**1777** Assembly Rooms complete. Henry Joy brings in cotton industry, and thus industrial revolution, replacing un-industrialised linen trade depressed by American War of Independence.

**1778** *John Paul Jones*, an American privateer, engages *HMS Drake* in Belfast Lough, inspiring Presbyterians to form 1st Volunteer Company seeking independence for Irish parliament.

**1791** Society of the United Irishmen is launched.

**1792** Boys at Belfast's Academy stage an armed insurrection.

**1795** The Orange Order is founded, and the United Irishmen's leader, Wolfe Tone, is captured.

**1796** US consulate established in Belfast.

**1798** Rebellion of Presbyterian-led United Irishmen is crushed. Henry Joy McCracken is hanged. Wexford revolt. Wolfe Tone commits suicide.

**1800** Act of Union dissolves Irish Parliament, creates United Kingdom of Great Britain and Ireland.

**1828** The decision is made to build Belfast's first power-driven linen mill.

**1832** Cholera epidemic. Hercules Street riots between Orangemen and Catholics mark the beginning of centuries of disturbances on 12 July.

**1839** Ulster Railway Company launched.

**1841** Riots ensue when Daniel 'the Liberator' O'Connell calls for repeal of the Act of Union.

**1845** Charles Lanyon refurbishes Belfast Exchange, launching his architectural career.

**1846** Famine victims flock to Belfast. Typhus ensues. Soup kitchens open.

**1847** Orangemen burn Daniel O'Connell's effigy on news of his death. Riots follow, with Protestant shipwrights fighting Catholic navvies. More violent riots two years later.

**1849** Queen Victoria pays a visit, but the city corporation mis-spells the Irish for 'Hundred Thousand Welcomes'. Cholera strikes.

**1857** July's sectarian riots put down by Hussars.

**1863** Harland & Wolff launches *Alexandria*. Gallagher's Tobacco factory opened.

**1887** First pneumatic tyre invented in Belfast.

**1888** Belfast receives royal charter as a city.

**1892** Home Rule (for Ireland) Bill defeated.

**1907** Big Jim Larkin's arrival electrifies Dock Strike, uniting Catholic and Protestant artisans.

**1912** The *Titanic*, Belfast built and designed, sinks. On 28 September, 471,414 predominantly Protestant Ulsterfolk sign Solemn League and Covenant opposing impending Home Rule.

**1913** 100,000 Covenantors join Ulster Volunteer Force under rebel British general. A (Unionist) provisional government is devised. British navy to blockade Belfast. Irish-based British officers mutiny. Arms for the UVF arrive by the ton.

**1914** World War I saves Ulster from civil war.

**1916** Dublin's Easter Rising, inspired by Belfast wing of Irish Republican Brotherhood, is suppressed. In the war, the Ulster Division loses 5,000 men on the Somme battlefield on 1 July.

**1920** Recession fires riots, curbed by curfew.

**1921** Six counties of Northern Ireland remain in the UK as rest of the island becomes 26-county Irish Free State, renaming itself as Éire in 1937 declaring its neutrality in World War II, and becoming the Republic of Ireland in 1949.

**1932** Unemployment following Wall Street crash, provokes city riots.

**1941** German bombing of Belfast. 700 dead.

**1956** Ineffectual six year IRA campaign begins.

**1968–9** Civil rights marches suppressed. Civil unrest worsens. British troops intervene.

**1971** The Chichesters finally bow out as James Chichester Clark, the Prime Minister, resigns.

**1972** 13 demonstrators are shot dead by British paratroopers on 'Bloody Sunday' in Londonderry. Parliament in Belfast is abolished and direct rule from Westminster is imposed. More than 3,000 will die violently in the next 20 years.

**1994** First IRA 'ceasefire'. Similar 'declarations' from most Protestant paramilitaries.

**1996** IRA ends ceasefire with London bombing.

**1997** Second IRA 'ceasefire'.

**1998** 71 percent of voters back self-governing all-party Assembly, but terrorists refuse to hand in weapons, slowing the peace process.

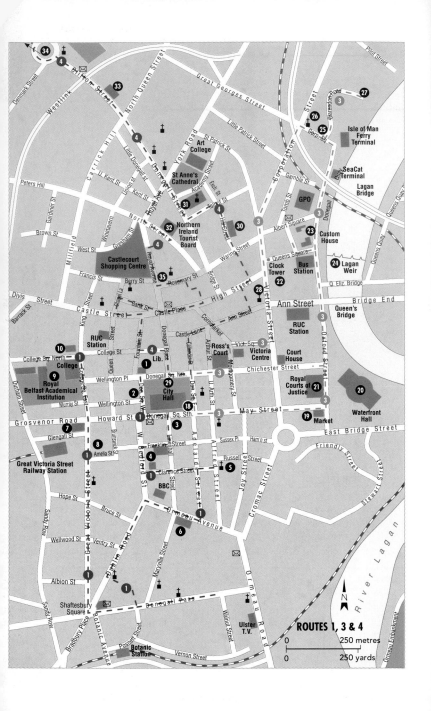

# Route 1

## The Linen town

**Linen Hall Library – Heroes' Heads – Linen Conservation Area – Ulster Hall – Group Theatre – Ormeau Baths Gallery – Golden Mile – Cirque & Grand Opera House – Crown Liquor Saloon – Old Museum**

The first route starts at the Linen Hall Library, explores the warehouse architecture of the Linen Conservation Area south of City Hall, visiting halls of entertainment, theatres and art galleries while offering detours east to St Malachy's Church and the antique shops of Donegall Pass, before turning north again for the Victorian charms of the Cirque & Grand Opera House plus the Crown Liquor Saloon.

On Donegall Square North the ★★ **Linen Hall Library** ❶ (Monday to Wednesday and Friday 9.30am–5.30pm, Thursday 9.30am–8.30pm, Saturday 9.30am–4pm) is one of the few public-subscription libraries left in these islands. It was founded by the Belfast Reading Society, later to become the Belfast Society for Promoting Knowledge, at the beginning of a radical decade which culminated in the 1798 Rebellion of the United Irishmen. Thomas Russell, a founder member and its first librarian, was arrested at its original premises in Ann Street for his part in the uprising and his life, which ended on the scaffold at Downpatrick Gaol, is commemorated in the ballad *The Man From God Knows Where*. The Library's second location was in the White Linen Hall (where it was the linen that was white, not the hall).

But, by the first centenary of the rebellion, that hall had been demolished and the library had moved across the street to Nos. 16–18 Donegall Square North, a three-storey five-bay linen warehouse with stucco mouldings to its windows and a chamfered corner on to Fountain Street. The building had been designed by Charles Lanyon (*see page 61*) as a linen warehouse of greyish-yellowish brick with a dressing of Victorian detail upon its Georgian proportions. The swags and folds of linen drapery around its doorway, pinned back by rosettes and by the Red Hand of Ulster upon a shield, are prime clues to its origins.

Inside, an impressive brass-railed stone staircase leads to the muted calm of arcane reading rooms redolent with the aromas of the book stacks, the walls lined with heavy wooden glass-fronted bookcases and the stained-glass windows commemorating famous writers. While old men turn broadsheet newspaper pages, the obsessive pursue their eclectic researches, and bookish conversation is whispered over tea and scones in its café's Edwardian

*Linen Hall Library*

**15**

*The library's café*

*Scottish Provident Institution and sculpture of indigenous North American*

atmosphere among temporary displays of maps and etchings often for sale. The library's collection of Irish books is exceptional and it has continued in its radical position, holding over 80,000 items of catalogued ephemera representing all political opinions concerned in the 30 years of the Troubles, a treasurehouse for historians and political journalists.

Free day-passes are readily dispensed, though gaining a place on the Society's Board of Governors is a trifle more difficult. Aspirants can, literally, be blackballed if an existing Governor drops a black, rather than a white, marble into the tin porringer passed round at elections.

Carvings high up on the pale Giffock sandstone of the vast **Scottish Provident Institution ❷**, stretching south along Donegall Square West, attest to the city's industrial heritage. The building has almost as much Edwardian pomp and presence as the City Hall (*see page 37*) it borders. Cherubs work at their ABCs on a Gutenberg printing press and easily identified are an anchor and hammer for shipbuilding, plus skeins of linen yarn and spinning wheel, the tools of ropemaking. Below, less finely carved heads, copied from Thomas Fitzpatrick's work on the McCausland Building in Victoria Street (*see page 36*), represent the peoples to which a commercially buoyant city exported its goods: an Englishman, benign and plump; an Asian tribal chief with his nose-ring; a thick-lipped African; an indigenenous north American with high cheekbones. Further non-PC stereotypes may be obscured by insensitive shop frontages. Here the famous Ulster greatcoat, as worn by Sherlock Holmes, was first tailored. Here the celebrated architect Charles Lanyon had his offices.

**Yorkshire House ❸**, on the corner of Donegall Square South and Linen Hall Street, was built in 1862 as a three-storey, 18-bay linen warehouse. The pert-breasted nymph on high in the first niche on Linen Hall Street, plus the **Heroes' Heads** between first-floor windows – gravity's Newton, the current's Humboldt, the loom's Jacquard, electricity's Watt, steam's Stevenson, poetry's Tom Moore, M'langelo (*sic*), Shakspeare (*sic*), Schiller, Homer, Columbus and Washington plus the gods Minerva, Flora and Mercury – attest to the wide aspirations of entrepreneurial spirits of the time. Its abutting extension is Lancashire House, both sides in the War of The Roses now united.

*Linen Hall Street*

**Linen Hall House** at Nos. 13–19 Linen Hall Street, built in 1855, spent much of its life serving the linen trade, as did No. 40, and to the right in Franklin Street, Nos. 25–27. Turning left, it is easy to spot the sometimes polychrome one-time linen warehouses on ever so windy Bedford Street, particularly the warm brown sandstone mass of **Ewart House** (No. 17), built as the Italian Renaissance palace for a linen dynasty, and the lesser brick *palazzi* at Nos. 21–25, 27–33 (once the Emerald Shirt Company), 35 37, 34–44, 46–50 and 58–60.

The welcoming folk at No. 28, **Bryson House** – designed in 1865 for the linen trade by Lanyon's great rival W.J. Barre (*see page 61*) in a riot of seductive detail emulating a townhouse for a Venetian count – are employed by a range of voluntary arts and social organisations.

The eclectic Barre also designed the more restrained two-storey Italianate stucco next door of the ★★ **Ulster Hall ❹** (tel: 028-9032 3900 for access outside performance times). Completed in 1862 as a grand ballroom, it became the largest music hall in these islands, its airy spaciousness and excellent acoustics also providing a resounding platform for the rallies of the Irish Nationalist politicians Charles Stewart Parnell and Patrick Pearse and one holding the opposite view, David Lloyd George who later became British Prime Minister. Now it is a regular venue for entertainments as varied as the Ulster Orchestra's Friday concerts, boxing matches, jazz gigs, ethnic sessions, craft fair days and contemporary political grandstanding. Cult rockers will know that the Rolling Stones played the Hall in 1964 and that Led Zeppelin's *Stairway to Heaven* had its stage debut here in 1971. The Hall's massive Mulholland organ attracts the differently dedicated.

*Irish dancing*

The portraits over the round windows are of bewhiskered local worthies, and the scurrilous have suggested that the convex bow to the balcony accommodates the aldermanic paunch.

The attached **Group Theatre** (access and programme tel: 028 9032 9685), once the Ulster's Minor Hall, a promenade area for *flâneurs* and stage-door Johnnies, was, at the start of the 20th century, home to the Ulster Literary Theatre which transferred many productions to the

National Theatre Society's Abbey Theatre in Dublin and to London's West End. The actor Stephen Boyd, whose camp Messala was Charlton Heston's rival in the 1959 version of *Ben-Hur*, learned his trade here.

However, in 1959 the resident company fell foul of the Unionist-dominated City Hall's heavy-handed political censorship of Sam Thompson's anti-sectarian polemic *Over The Bridge*, so that nowadays professional productions are rare. Nevertheless, the tiny venue is the unofficial base for the province's amateurs, who concentrate on provincial farce and revivals of Rutherford Mayne's *The Drone* and Gerald Macnamara's *Thompson in Tir-na-n'Og*, upon which the theatre's success was founded.

*Group Theatre performance of 'Things that are Caesar's', 1946*

**18**

Turning left takes us into Clarence Street, which was originally named Henrietta Street after one of the Lady Donegalls, with the dusky red-brick exterior of the Roman Catholic ★★ **St Malachy's Church ❺** (tel: 028-9032 1713) framed in the east. Designed by Thomas Jackson in 1880, this church, romantic as a Sir Walter Scott novel, is a splendid, octagonally turreted castellated excursion into Tudor Gothic, its panelled door studded and topped with armorial shields.

However, it is the church's interior that makes the stranger gasp. The dazzling ★★ **fan-vaulted ceiling**, a confection of creamy and frothy plasterwork, has been likened to a wedding cake turned inside out. In fact, it is an echo of Henry VII's Chapel in Westminster Abbey. Many of the original unpolished Irish oak fittings have disappeared but the organ is a century and a half old.

Built on the edge of Chapel Fields, home to mountebanks and cut-purses even into the 1930s, the church's chief benefactor, Captain Thomas Griffiths, understood that it would become the city's Roman Catholic cathedral,

*St Malachy's church: the fan-vaulted ceiling*

which accounts for the extravagance of decoration. A memorial to Griffiths is just inside the porch. The oak spire has long since been demolished, the original bell from the front left turret cracked and melted down. A new bell installed in 1868 no longer tolls, for its resonance was claimed to interfere with the maturing of spirit in Dunville's Whiskey Distillery, which stood nearby.

Return west up Clarence Street, a glimpse of the Black Mountain in the distance, to take the second left south along Linen Hall Street, emerging on to Ormeau Avenue where the city's reservoir once shimmered. Much of the south side of the Avenue was destroyed during the Troubles, the warehouse sites now turned into car parks, but Nos. 5, 9, 11, 13 and 17 are still recognisable as the linen-finishing houses they once were. Indeed, so famous was the Franklin Steam Laundry at No. 13 that customers from across Great Britain posted their linen shirts there to have cuffs and collars starched and pressed.

*Ormeau Baths Gallery*

The BBC's Broadcasting House is on the right, the low Queen Anne red-brick elegance of the ★★ **Ormeau Baths Gallery** ◗ (Tuesday to Saturday 9.30am–5.30pm) opposite. Originally the Ormeau Avenue Public Baths, its eastern half became the city's premier visual arts space in 1995. Inexplicably the plug has been pulled on every visual vestige of public ablutions, but the resultant four bright, white, airy arts spaces now play host, under young director Hugh Mulholland, to contemporary Irish and touring art, sometimes accessible, sometimes confrontational.

Almost unnoticed at the junction of Ormeau Avenue and Bedford Street, shaded under dusty trees, stands the **Thomas Thompson Memorial**, erected in memory of the founder of the city's Home for the Incurable. It takes the form of an elaborate crusty red Aberdeen granite and sandstone drinking fountain bearing the legend 'Who so drinketh of the water that I shall give him'. Thompson, a naval surgeon during the Napoleonic Wars, served in Latin America and the West Indies, gaining knowledge that led to his publication, in 1832, of *Practical Remarks on the Epidemic of Cholera, which at Present Prevails in Belfast and its Vicinity*. Smallpox, dysentery and typhus were his other adversaries in the 1840s Famine.

Bankmore Street, to the south, running parallel to the Avenue, offers alternative health risks as the locus of a tiny alfresco red-light industry.

Among the medieval-style heads carved below the spire of Thompson's fountain is one of the good doctor himself, sporting Dundreary whiskers and monocle. Since the fountain is now dry, perhaps a break is called for in **Morrison's Spirit Grocers** opposite, an entirely ersatz but enticing conglomeration of Edwardiana evoking an Ireland of the past, where beer engine and ham slicer – and often barber's razor and undertaker's wringing hands – were all wielded on the same premises.

'All that glisters is not gold' is a poetic aphorism well remembered along the Dublin Road. Running south towards Shaftesbury Square, it was dubbed (too generously) **The Golden Mile** in the darkest hours of the Troubles when its only night-time strollers were as likely to have been assassins, spies, bombers, police, SAS undercover patrols or journalists as honest revellers. It is now, by early evening, a useful assemblage of Ireland's interpretation of brasserie and bistro, ethnic eateries, pizza parlours, pubs, restaurants and fast-food joints. By midnight, pubbers and clubbers jostle across street and pavement, making passageway, even by taxi, almost impossible. By day, charity shops and fashionable furniture emporiums add to the attractions.

*Dublin Road*

**20**

Once the Elbow Room stood at No. 3, a public house of some style for almost a century and a half and, in the 1950s and 1960s, the heart of literary Belfast, casting couch and alternative studio for long-lunching BBC producers. But there are few echoes of the original in the new Elbow Room incorporated into the Dempsey's Terrace entertainment complex at No. 45. Willis House at No. 25 commemorates William Willis, who invented the commercial immersion heater there.

The headquarters of the Orange Order, the **Grand Orange Lodge of Ireland**, is at No. 65. Inkermann Terrace, Nos. 73–83, is named after a fort besieged during the Crimean War where, in 1854, 12,000 British and French repelled an attacking force of 40,000 Russians. The nearby Shaftesbury Square Reformed Presbyterian Church dates from 1890.

**Shaftesbury Square**, named after the 7th Earl of Shaftesbury, is a desolate place, day or night. Plastic bags and discarded fast-food cartons, Ireland's tumbleweed, bumble wind-blown from Donegall Pass to the old Art Deco basement public toilets (soon to be a restaurant) amid undistinguished and unappealing buildings. A left turn leads to a rich and rare blend of fascinating antique shops and motorbike salesrooms in **Donegall Pass**, the streets off it named after the trees in the wood it passed through. Pianist Barry Douglas passed through No. 99, the School of Music. One of the notoriously sadistic Magdalene Asylums for 'erring and repentant females' stood behind the sandstone parish church at No. 54.

*Service in the Roscoff*

Yet the square has some delights, not least the fashionable chrome-chaired **Roscoff** restaurant, flagship of a new age in contemporary Belfast cuisine (*see page 68*). High up on the **Ulster Bank**'s Portland stone at the cor-

ner of Dublin Road and Great Victoria Street there are also
two of the best public art pieces in Northern Ireland. These
floating ★ **bronze figures** by the sculptor Elizabeth Frink
have been dubbed Draft and Overdraft by a public who already called this end wall Clark's Gable after the Bank's
then director. (This is characteristic Ulster humour.)

*The Bank's bronze figures*

Now proceeding north, the route follows **Great Victoria Street**, once an avenue of fine red-brick and stucco ter-
raced houses. But the bombers of the 1970s continued what
the planners had only in part achieved a decade earlier: the
demotion of its southern half to a mix of derelict lots, car
parks, brutal 1960s constructions, advertising hoardings
and an unfortunate four-lane cross-highway. Ambitious
plans to resuscitate its social cachet are, at the time of
going to press, still on the drawing board.

Now little but the ice cream-coloured stucco styling
of the 1860s Great Victoria Street **Presbyterian Church**
and the upper storeys of Victorian Richmond Terrace, just
north of the Christian Science Reading Rooms north of
the Ulster Bank, remain to tell of its former dignity. Across
the road is the entirely rebuilt Apostolic Evangelical Pen-
tacostal Church, in the 1870s, the city's first synagogue.
Vere Foster, the revolutionary educational philanthropist
who helped many to America in the Famine years, lived
and died at No. 115. A print gallery operates from No. 125.

*Great Victoria Street facade*

The polychrome brick building on the terrace's town
side, Shaftesbury Square Hospital designed by W. J. Barre
in 1867, originally cared for those with ophthalmic prob-
lems and more latterly for those suffering another kind
of darkness, substance abuse.

Designed by Ian Campbell, Fanum House, grey,
Lubianka like, forbidding, stands to the north where
Grattan & Co, in 1825, first manufactured aerated waters,
founding an industry in which local firm Cantrell &
Cochrane is still among the world's leaders.

Water was also a concern of the painter Paul Henry's
father, minister at the Great Victoria Street Baptist Church
on the corner of Hope Street. He scandalised his 1870 congregation by announcing he had lost faith in total-
immersion baptism. The tiny house abutting is claimed as
the city's narrowest. To the west, the pagodas of the White-
hall Tobacco Works rise in front of the Black Mountain.

*The Grand Opera House*

Little in Nos. 20–30, Chamber of Commerce House,
commemorates those of its founding members who were
active among the United Irishmen in the 1798 rebellion.

But the street's honeypot is the ★★★ **Cirque & Grand
Opera House** ❼ (Opera House Experience tours by
arrangement, ticket shop 2–4 Great Victoria Street, tel:
028-9024 1919). Designed by Frank Matcham, it is an ori-
ental fantasy of minaret and pediment where even the

*A riot of crimson and gold*

*Crown Liquor Saloon and detail*

ventilation lantern has a Moorish air to it. On the corner of Great Victoria Street and Glengall Street, where the Ulster Unionist Party has its headquarters, this palace of varieties and delights is a little dwarfed by the Europa, the self-proclaimed most bombed (43 times) hotel in western Europe, from whose comforts three decades of reporters covered the Troubles. To its left, fronting the entrance to the Europa BusCentre and Rail Station, pose Louise Walsh's two clothed life-sized tributes to low-paid working women opposite Amelia Street, once the bordello area.

High on the Opera House a naked bronze Mercury takes flight and Shakespeare looks down approvingly while the conservatory crush bar, added during renovations, seems quite appropriate. However, it is the interior which really delights, a riot of crimson and gold leaf with gilded elephant heads supporting the boxes and a heavenly ceiling mural added by Cherith, wife to Robert McKinstry who carried out the major restoration of a near-abandoned building. Two IRA bombs caused further damage in the 1990s but by then the city had recognised the worth of an artistic flagship where Sarah Bernhardt, Orson Welles, and Laurel and Hardy had trod the boards, and the splendid auditorium is now regular host to touring Shakespeares, opera, ballet and post-West End musicals. Van Morrison's *Live at the Grand Opera House* was recorded there in 1984.

Across the street, and linked (allegedly) by a tunnel allowing stage-door Johnnies to cozy chorus girls in its private snugs, is another riot of the Victorian Baroque, the ★★★ **Crown Liquor Saloon ❽**, a bar now preserved by the National Trust. Once the Ulster Railway Hotel, dating from the same year as the Opera House, it was also restored by McKinstry. It is a cream, three-storey stucco building whose ground-floor bar is lavishly tiled in many

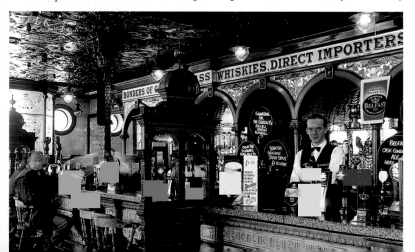

colours and whose snugs – with bronze match strikers and a bell that wags a flag to summon service – are guarded by griffin and lion.

The ceiling is embossed, the oysters and Guinness admirable, the waiters amenable and the customers a mixed bunch of stage hands, actors, journalists, travel writers, students and open-mouthed tourists sometimes too overcome to call their order for a pint. Upstairs, panels from the *Britannic*, the *Titanic*'s sister-ship, adorn an Irish theme bar. James Mason's haunted, hunted IRA man seeks sanctuary in a perfect replica of the Crown in Carol Reed's nightmarish 1947 film noir classic *Odd Man Out*, scripted from his own novel by Belfast-based F. L. Green.

**Robinson's Bar**, two doors north, was fire-bombed in 1991 but has been rebuilt, its exterior faithfully, to the original 1846 design, its interior given over to a whimsy of theme bars such as Fibber Magee's which opts for the full range of spirit grocer's artefacts. A beaten docket is a failed betting slip, the jokey name for the Irish theme pub that faces the Crown across Amelia Street (although its interior is pure 1985).

Diagonally opposite from the Grand Opera House, across Fisherwick Place, is the rusticated sandstone Tudor Gothic bulk of the **Presbyterian Assembly Rooms**, the essential Englishness of its mullioned windows made dour by Scots corbelling and a crown spire copied from St Giles' Cathedral, Edinburgh. The doorway arch and oriel window above are carved with biblical burnishing bushes and 14 angels 'specially copied from life'. The contest for its design in 1899 was clouded in unbiblical scandal, however, the winner being the Church's own architect who devised the competition. The exterior turret clock was the first in these islands to use electricity to drive its cogs and to ring its 12-bell carillon of 28 tunes.

Now the ground floor is given over to shops, and the majestically polygonal Assembly Room upstairs, still one of the most impressive venues in Belfast, can be leased for concert, pantomime and such.

College Square takes its name from the fine square lawn that was to surround the Georgian symmetry of the long, three-storey dusky red brick of the **+ + Royal Belfast Academical Institution** **N**, just north of Jury's Hotel opposite the Assembly Rooms. Now set beyond lawns much reduced, its spare elegance owing much to the 1807 designs by that great English architect Sir John Soane, it is the city's finest building. However, debts forced the Governors to sell off land on which was built, in five storeys of Portland stone, the Municipal Technical Institute, now the **Belfast Institute** (a.k.a. the College of Knowledge). Its style is pompous Baroque Revivalist, its four copper

*Presbyterian Assembly Rooms*

*Royal Belfast Academical Institution (above) and the Belfast Institute*

domed turrets are impressive and the city's coat of arms is set above the main doorway.

But the loss of green sward, and the education of rude labourers, destroyed College Square East and North, and the square's cachet as *the* address for surgeons and academics – the physicist Lord Kelvin was born in No. 17 East. The tall houses soon fell, first to commerce, then to the bomb. Only the block containing, at No. 7 College Square North, the **Old Museum** , a Greek Revival building of the 1830s, attests to former glories. The Belfast Natural History Society, which still owns the place, engaged architect Thomas Jackson to erect this chaste building, modelling it on the Choragic Monument of Thrasyllus with its portico replicating that of Athens' tower of Andronicus and its upper portions the Temple of Minerva.

*The Old Museum*

Inside, on the ground floor of what is now called the **Old Museum Arts Centre** (O'Mac to its friends), are a café and an appealing art gallery devoted to post-feminist issues. Upstairs is a 100-seat theatre favouring cutting-edge productions, while the galleried top floor seems frozen in the days when the museum's director described his occupation as 'curator and bird stuffer'. A scheme to rescue the adjoining abandoned houses is under way.

Fans can only gaze across at the space where No. 36 stood, serving originally as a Royal Irish Constabulary barracks, much later the Maritime Club where Van Morrison and Them first raised the roof with *G.L.O.R.I.A.*

*Reverend Dr Henry Cooke*

The return to the Linen Hall Library is via Wellington Place, passing the '**Black Man**' on his plinth. This 1876 statue of rabble-rousing Presbyterian cleric the Reverend Dr Henry Cooke is not actually black but of green bronze. The original figure, curiously painted black and later moved to the City Hall, was of the 1885 Earl of Belfast. The reverend, whom Daniel O'Connell – 'The Liberator' to Nationalists in the mid-19th century – referred to as 'Bully Cooke', has his back turned to the Academy whose visionary notions on equality and radical science he desperately opposed. An alternative approach to the Library is via the artists' studios of King's and Queen's streets, and then College Street, whose offshoot, **College Court**, was named Squeeze-Gut Entry in the 18th century. The view north is of Cave Hill, its ridge profile dubbed Napoleon's Nose by citizens mocking the 1798 rebellion and cocking a snoot at the aggressive emperor (*see page 46*).

Only Nos. 7–11 of the original 1830 houses in **Wellington Place** remain. Now a street of building societies and assurance companies, it was named after the Duke of Wellington, who spent much of his boyhood at Annadale in the south of the city. The shopfront of No. 58 is one of the few examples in Belfast of Art Nouveau.

## Route 2

*The Botanic Gardens with the Palm House*

**Dreaming Spires**

**Crescent Arts Centre – Crescent Gardens – Queen's University – Elmwood Hall – Ulster Museum – Royal Botanic Gardens – Union Theological College**

A stroll through the University area, stopping off at a former inspiration for artists and poets and an oasis which still inspires lovers and rocks to summer concerts.

Unlovely **Shaftesbury Square** lies at the northern apex of the University quarter, an appealing area of mid range hotels, inexpensive B&Bs, lively student pubs, tree-lined thoroughfares and busy bistros in the shadow of church and academic spires and resonant to the stanzas of so many of Ireland's acclaimed contemporary poets.

First look west up Donegall Road for a fine view of Black Hill, then duck down Albion Lane and enter the Cobbles, the rear entrance to **Lavery's Gin Palace**. During the 1950s and 1960s this was haven for artists and poets including William Conor, John Hewitt and Louis MacNeice, and indeed some who favoured revolution in the heady days of 1968 seem to have lingered on, sipping pints, tucking into inexpensive trencherman lunches, placing bets in the adjoining bookmaker's office. It is also one of the few bars where town still meets gown.

*Directions around Queen's*

Emerge east through the Gin Palace's front door (Nos. 12–14) past the bouncers, turning left and south along **Bradbury Place**. Among its few surviving 19th-century buildings are a distraction of multinational fast-food outlets, its pavements deep in their seemingly inevitable detritus from early evening onwards. **Bishop's** is a tiled haven of traditional fish 'n' chips and, at Nos. 40–42 **Tom**

*The Crescent Arts Centre*

*... and neigbouring church*

*Mortar Board Christian Café*

**Caldwell** specialises in expensive furniture and contemporary Irish art in his eponymous gallery, while across the road is the **M-Club**, glitzy dance venue where the weekend's highlight is the appearance of minor celebrities from British television's soaps.

Further south, past No. 48's octagonal Art Deco weathercock-topped gazebo and over the railway bridge, into the ★ **University Conservation Area**, there stands at the corner of University Road and Lower Crescent the 1873 Scrabo stone Scots baronial pile that is the **Crescent Arts Centre** ⓫. This maze of rooms and studios is noted for its devotion to New Age diversions, Latin American gigs, eclectic theatre and the excellent contemporary ★ **art gallery** run by its eponymous Persian philosopher Jamshid Mirfenderesky. The centre runs an intriguing literary festival, *Between The Lines*, each spring.

Across University Road is tiny **King William Park**, commemorated in Frank Ormsby's ironic poem of the same name, where William III hitched his horse in 1690. Its southern neighbours are topped by the pinnacled spire of the 1887 **Moravian church** and the campanile of the **Wesleyan chapel**, designed by W.J. Barre, which would not look out of place in Lombardy. The Crescent Centre's neighbour is the **Crescent Church**, charismatic in its worship, French medieval in its architectural inspiration, God's light shining through its pierced campanile.

But our route nips east behind the church past the grand pilasters of the stuccoed Georgian terraces of **Lower Crescent** with a nod to the bar-flies in **The Fly**, a public house familiar to those familiar with the work of poet Ciarán Carson, before dodging the winos in otherwise pleasant **Crescent Gardens** ⓬, once a potato patch, to join imposing Upper Crescent and University Road. Moving south we pass the pleasant stucco and Doric porticos of **Mount Charles**, once home to novelist Forrest Reid and poet John Hewitt. At the top of University Street, Presbyterian and Church of Ireland spires come into view, well east.

Across the road are three Georgian rows, Prospect Terrace, Botanic View and Cinnamond's Buildings, plus the Victorian stucco and Georgian brick terraces of Camden and Fitzwilliam Streets. These, respectively, were home ground for Brian Moore's *The Lonely Passion of Judith Hearne* and Nobel Laureate poet Seamus Heaney's campus flat, where the **Mortar Board Christian Café** now stands. **Tank**, an avant-garde gallery, operates from a mews further down Fitzwilliam.

Next comes Georgian **University Square** where several houses – now University departments – sport magnolia in their gardens. The Church of Ireland's Canon

Hannay (1865–1950) a.k.a. George A. Birmingham, the nationalistic author of 60-plus satirical novels, lived at No. 75 University Road, the painter Paul Henry at No. 61.

Charles Lanyon designed the pleasingly mellowed dusty-red brick facade of ★★★ **Queen's University** ⓭, shamelessly appropriating the lines of the Founder's Tower at Magdalen College, Oxford, for its central feature. The university was first named Queen's College after the young Victoria when she laid the foundation stone in 1845. As suited the hierarchical nature of the times, the architect provided lavish accommodations for Chancellors and other dignitaries while offering the students little except four water closets and a row of urinals. Off the soaring entrance hall, during term time, are the Great Hall's inexpensive lunching facilities, an **Information Centre** keeping office hours and a restful cloistered quadrangle beyond which lies the Seamus Heaney Library.

*Queen's University*

To the left, the **Old Library** is easily identified as a Gothic gargoyled edifice from Lanyon's studio. The Whitla Hall to the right is used for concerts during the November run of the three-week **Belfast Festival at Queen's**, directed from 25 College Gardens (tel: 028-9066 7687) nearby.

27

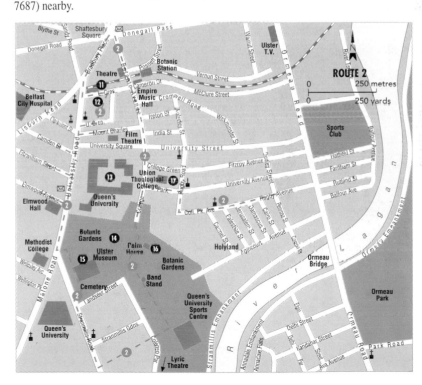

*Elmwood Hall*

*Lord Kelvin*

*Ulster Museum exterior*

Opposite the University's lawns stand its grim Student's Union and the delightful Italianate deconsecrated wedding cake which, as **Elmwood Hall**, is another festival venue and home to the Ulster Orchestra. Above its three-tiered Presbyterian spire a gilt weathercock catches the sun. The **University Bookshop** adjoins.

Further down Elmwood Avenue is a Non-Subscribing Presbyterian spire and what is now the Catholic Chaplaincy, from where the poet Philip Larkin wrote many of his finest lines. Beyond again is the **Elmwood Gallery**, the public face of the private Ulster Arts Club.

South of the University, past Methodist College on the right, the road divides into Malone and Stranmillis, the former an expanse of leafy avenues that spell middle-class achievement. Stranmillis Road, by contrast, has an off-campus feel to it, so our route left enters the gates of the ★★★ **Royal Botanic Gardens** ⑭ (open daylight hours), by its 1912 statue to Lord Kelvin, formulator of the Second Law of Thermodynamics. Students make free with jokes concerning his two accompanying metal spheres.

To the right, through the fir trees of the sombre pinetum, is the splendid ★★★ **Ulster Museum** ⑮ (tel: 028-9038 3000, open Monday to Friday 10am–5pm, Saturday 1–5pm, Sunday 2–5pm; admission free), once the municipal Art Gallery. Now Irish art from the Bronze Age to the contemporary is well presented, and travelling exhibitions open other windows. Other floors concentrate on the island's biological, geological, industrial and social heritages. Most enduringly popular are artefacts rescued from the Spanish Armada galleass *Gerona*, sunk off the north coast. Replicas for sale in the museum shop include a slim gold ring bearing the poignant admission *No tengo mas que dar te* (I have nothing more to give you).

Leaving the museum, go uphill past the cholera mound and Victorian angels of Friar's Bush Cemetery, dating, not from a spurious AD483 tombstone but from a 16th-century friary. Away to the left are views of the white bulk of Stormont on distant hills, ahead the bistros and hair snippers of Stranmillis village and the reliable **Lyric Theatre** where Liam Neeson first trod the boards.

Stranmillis Gardens leads back into Botanic Gardens where a northwestern course through roses and hedged walks sets fair for both ★ **Tropical Ravine** and ★★ **Palm House** ⑯ (tel: 028-9032 4902, closed 1–2pm; open April to September, Monday to Friday 10am–5pm, weekend 2–5pm; October to March, Monday to Friday 10am–4pm, weekend 2–4pm; admission free). In the 1889 ravine, water drips from banana leaves in a miniature sunken rainforest while palm fronds form exotic patterns against the glass dome of the Palm House, executed 50 years earlier by iron-founder Richard Turner to Lanyon's designs. Once the garden's entertainments edified tradesmen, now U2 rocks, Bob Dylan mesmerises and Van Morrison lyricises in summer concerts, while students cram, lovers entwine and dogs can't read the No Ball Games notices.

*Concert in the Gardens*

Beyond the Palm House the north gate leads on to College Park and Botanic Avenue, while an optional diversion via the east gate takes you first through a district of neat red-brick terraces and a profligacy of churches known as the **Holy Land** because so many of its street names derive from biblical cities. Padraic Fiacc's poems have their homes here. Ahead is the formidable Scrabo stone mass of the ★ **Union Theological College** , its colonnaded facade by Lanyon. Persuasive charm gains entry to the impressive colonnaded and domed **library**, used by Northern Ireland's House of Commons while it awaited Stormont's completion. Its Senate sat in the chapel.

The city's arthouse cinema, the **Queen's Film Theatre**, is tucked away up University Square Mews, and the houses of Botanic Avenue retain, on their 2nd and 3rd floors, evidence of their 1870s origins. Deemed Belfast's *Boul' Mich'* (Boulevard St Michel in Paris) by Seamus Heaney, it now carries itself with a raffish louche air, its tree-lined pavements fronting on to bookmakers, bookshops and brasseries, townhouse hotels, B&Bs, coffee bars, charity counters, world craft emporiums and launderettes. The Madison Hotel's bar could be off Barcelona's Ramblas.

*The Empire Music Hall*

The **Empire Music Hall** (tel: 028-9024 9276) – in a deconsecrated church – provides live music and Tuesday-night stand-up comedy. Across street and railway bridge the **Civic Arts Theatre** (tel: 028-9031 6900) offers up an unpredictable schedule of home-spun farce, amateur musicals and imported cutting-edge drama. Past Kingham Mission Church, and you are back at Shaftesbury Square.

*Madison's*

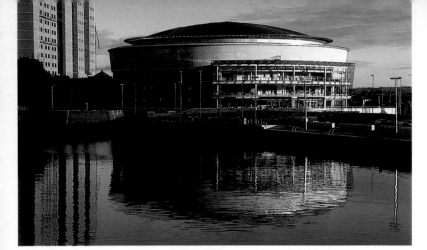

*Waterfront Hall*

## Route 3

Titanic Town

Titanic Memorial – St George's Market – Waterfront Hall – Courts – Albert Memorial Clock – Custom House – Harbour Office – Sinclair Seamen's Presbyterian Church – Clarendon Dock – Titanic's shipbuilder's statue *See map on page 14*

This route explores the city's links with the ill-fated liner and examines some more recent riverside developments, taking in Belfast's new cultural hub, the Waterfront Hall.

The sinking of the *Titanic* was a disaster that marked not just the ignominious end for a mighty liner but also the death throes of many of the old certitudes which divided the world into rulers and toilers and decreed that humans reigned supreme over nature.

*The Titanic's designer, Thomas Andrews, who went down with the ship (below) on its maiden voyage*

 *Titanic* conspiracy theorists claim that the greed of the ship's owners, the White Star Line, and the ensuing compromises made by its locally born designer Thomas Andrews, and the workmen of the Belfast shipyards who built it, were indirectly responsible for World War I. The theory goes that if Andrews had designed a better ship, coal would not have ignited spontaneously in its bunkers and stayed alight through its maiden voyage, weakening steel plate below the waterline, thus allowing the fatal iceberg to puncture so easily. The Mayday calls diverted the *Carpathia* which thus arrived in the Mediterranean port of Trieste two days late – but just in time to pick up, running down the dock, Gavrilo Princip, who was embarking for Fiume, on his way to assassinate the Archduke Ferdinand in Sarajevo. Douglas Carson of the **Titanic Trust**

(21 Cherry Valley, Belfast BT5 6JP, tel: 028-9079 4110) embellishes on this and other details.

In the grounds east of the City Hall at the base of the ★ **Titanic Memorial** two weeping sea-nymphs break the sea's cold grasp at the feet of a scantily clad marble statue of a female Fame, in their arms the Titanic's *Unknown Soldier*, an anonymous drowned man. An inscription in gold leaf records the names, including that of Andrews, of just 11 'gallant Belfast men who lost their lives on 15 April 1912 by the foundering of the Belfast-built *Titanic* through collision with an iceberg, on her maiden voyage from Southampton to New York'. But there is no mention of the dozens of doomed Belfast-born artisan crew and steerage-class passengers – or indeed of any women – on board. The 11 gallants comprised the shipyard's Guarantee Group, who were checking performance targets, even down to a reference to the superfluity of coat-hanger screws found in Andrews' notebook.

*Titanic memorial*

Nearby, an aggressive bronze figure in topee and puttees serves as a 1899–1902 **Boer War** cenotaph. The rock on which he stands is, as was the custom of the times, supported by two bare-breasted and two flimsily covered goddesses with pert *embonpoint*. Opposite, at Nos. 11–13 Donegall Square East, is a hexastyle Corinthian porticoed facade which is all that remains of the original once-grand 1840s **Methodist Church**. Its congregation long gone to the suburbs, its dull 1,500-seat auditorium transferred from God to Mammon and its fine box pews cannibalised for pubs and restaurants, it has been rebuilt as the Ulster Bank's corporate headquarters. Harry Ferguson designed the minimal-maintenance Ferguson tractor, revolutionising British farming, at Nos. 14–16. Other 19th-century shipbuilders lived at Nos. 18–20.

**May Street**, on the left, takes its name from the May family who curried society's favours, marrying Anna, an illegitimate daughter, to the second Marquis of Donegall. Although they became sovereigns of the city, the callous, snobbish marquis kept the marriage secret. A great linen warehouse by Lanyon once stood at the top of the street on the right, and another Lanyon creation, originally the Church of Ireland Diocesan Offices, in polychrome brick, still stands opposite.

*Riverside entertainers*

The rabble-rousing Reverend Henry Cooke preached in May Street's 1859 classically designed **Presbyterian Church**. It was, after all, built as a vehicle large enough to accommodate both his ego and his 1,700-strong congregation. Nevertheless, it refused Temperance meetings and gave serious consideration to a proposal to use its basement cemetery as a bonded whiskey warehouse. Inside there are impressive twin staircases, box pews, a mahogany gallery and fine timber coffered ceiling. To its east,

*Ross & Co*

*St George's Market*

*Waterfront Hall Interior*

towards the river, are the Doric columns of the church school. Almost opposite, Victoria Hall stands on the site of the Victoria Music Hall (built for amateur musicians) where, in 1882, a cornice fell, narrowly missing the novelist Charles Dickens while he was delivering a reading.

Along **Joy Street**, on the right, are the only surviving Georgian city-centre townhouses at ★ **Nos. 14–26**. Once red-brick merchants' homes, they were given over to theatrical lodgings and the street became known as the Street of Ps – Pride, Poverty and Pianos. Nos. 36–46 Hamilton Street have similar pasts.

Auctioneers **Ross & Co** occupy the souk-like caverns of Nos. 22–26, built in attractive brick and sandstone as the Presbyterian General Assembly's Office in 1875. Veterinary surgeon John Boyd Dunlop, says the plaque, invented the first successful pneumatic tyre at Nos. 38–42 and he ran a hospital for sick horses where Telephone House now stands at Nos. 43–71. Facing each other across the Cromac Street/May Street interface are two banks designed in the classical manner, both dating from 1919. The Ulster is distinguished by its Baroque cupola and a notice – whose history must lie in a long-forgotten staffing dispute – forbidding bicycles inside the building.

Beyond, on the corner with Verner Street, behind green faïence tiles, stands **Magennis's Whiskey Café & Public House**, picaresque local for Cromac Street horse dealers, traders from St George's Market and concert goers from the Waterfront Hall. The brick, stone and iron **Market House** (1890), sympathetically restored as ★★ **St George's Market** ⓳ to the original designs held on linen in City Hall, is all that is left of many such markets that peppered the Laganside end of May Street, in an area still known colloquially as The Markets.

Across the road in what is now Lanyon Place, where noisome, vibrant cattle, flax, fruit, grain, horse, pork, potato, fish and variety markets once thrived, are the spare sandy-coloured towers of the Hilton Hotel, a car park and British Telecom. These almost dwarf the stylishly emblematic ★★★ **Waterfront Hall** ⓴, whose flying-saucer contours, designed by Victor Robinson, bring many of the city's citizens their first close encounters with the once-alien world of ballet, concert, opera and tribute band. The hall's café-bars look upriver and at night, from Oxford Street, habitués seem as tiny as *ET* lounge lizards.

Beside the tiny Water Service Pumping Station, seven died and six times that number were badly injured in the 21 July 1972 IRA bus-stop bombing run that became known as Bloody Friday.

Across the street, west through iron security gates at the bottom of Chichester Street, stands the almost white imposing Portland stone neoclassical bulk of the

★★ **Royal Courts of Justice** ㉑ (tel: 028-9023 5111 for daily lists). Bewigged barristers and pinstriped solicitors parade, clutching pink-ribboned legal bundles while miscreants, plaintiffs and their accusers and pursuers seem (mostly) in awe of the travertine marble vastness of its echoing central hall. Opposite is the Old Town Hall completed in 1870, and now, after much bombing, restored as the **Belfast County Court** (tel: 028-9023 2721 for lists).

Downstream towards ★ **Queen's Bridge** –designed by Charles Lanyon, named after Queen Victoria and built of Newry granite to replace the old Long Bridge which had been *the* place in 1790 for an evening's *paseo,* stands a pedantic cream sandstone perpendicular diversion, once St Malachy's Schools. Beyond Anne Street along Donegall Quay, past a bistro that was once a ships' chandlers and **Laganside BusCentre**, is the city's potentially most appealing vista, ★ **Queen's Square** where, until the 1840s, ships tied up at quays named after the Donegall family. Here stands Ireland's answer to Pisa's leaning tower, topped by the 1-m (3-ft) out-of-plumb Gothic ★ **Albert Memorial Clock** ㉒. The 34-m (113-ft) column is named after Queen Victoria's stern consort, who is displayed in his Garter robes. Though Lanyon secretly joined the committee that chose its design, a decision to award him the contract was declared improper and the work went to his rival Barre.

*Queen's Bridge*

*Albert Memorial Clock*

The much-restored **McHugh's Bar**, on the left, claims to be Belfast's oldest extant building. Once a raffish wen of bordello taverns, it included Madame Du Barry's where painter Stanley Spencer supped while his brother Gilbert 'Professor' Spencer played cat-house piano in the 1940s.

Across the square is another of Lanyon's solid accomplishments in Portland stone, rich in Ionic and Doric columns. Built in 1852 for the Northern Bank it is the ★ **First Trust Bank**. Beyond, to the north in Custom House Square, is another tilted monument, the **Calder Fountain**, paid for and named after the founder of what became the Ulster Society for the Prevention of Cruelty to Animals. But the glory here goes to the magnificent Palladian simplicity of the ★★★ **Custom House** ㉓, the very zenith of Lanyon's achievements. Its real delight is a **pediment** of Britannia, Mercury and Neptune flanked by lion and unicorn, amid capstans and knots, executed by the great stonemason Thomas Fitzpatrick and seen best from the Lagan Lookout (*see over the page*). The novelist **Anthony Trollope** worked in the Custom House as a post office official in the 1850s.

**33**

*The Custom House*

Now our attention turns to the river. The Laganside Corporation was set up by the state with a mission to reclaim, revitalise and gentrify the Lagan's banks, an area on which

*Lagan Lookout Visitor Centre*

*Riverside redevelopment*

for so long the city had turned its back. First of its conquests had to be the river itself, little more than a mephitic cess of human and industrial effluent, torpid and foul smelling, exposing its detritus-despoiled mudbanks in spring-tide days, dangerous and threatening when its flash-flood storm drains proved less than adequate.

And so a massive purification scheme began. Tributaries were re-culverted, banks dredged and, where previous weirs had ironically served to maximise and retain tidal silting, the new scheme keeps the stream clear, welcoming back plopping grey mullet, the occasional homing Atlantic salmon and increasing numbers of wild brown trout. It also maintains a satisfactory water level upstream of ★★ **Lagan Weir ㉔** whose **Lagan Lookout Visitor Centre** (April to September Monday to Friday 11am–5pm, Saturday noon–5pm, Sunday 2–5pm; October to March Tuesday to Friday 11am–3.30pm, Saturday 1–4.30pm, Sunday 2–4.40pm) explains the river's long history. After dusk, blue lighting romanticises the structure.

The Corporation has devised an attractive ★★ **Riverside Walk** which follows the river upstream from the weir all the way to the Ormeau Bridge and back along the East Bank (*see Leisure, page 71*). Just downstream of the weir is pedestrianised **Donegall Quay**, with its massive riverwall, bordered on one side with jetties and slipways, on the other by practical but ornamental stone paviours and square-setts pierced by black bollards bearing the gilt seahorse from the city's coat of arms.

North along Donegall Quay, past the SeaCat terminal, is **Corporation Square** with its elegant sandstone ★★ **Harbour Office ㉕** decked out by Lanyon's partner W. H. Lynn. Its boardroom, which hosts the captain's table and chairs destined for the *Titanic* but completed too late for the voyage, is rich in fine historical paintings, including one of Captain Pirrie, grandfather to William, whose expansionist vision gave birth to the doomed liner. These riches can be inspected on request (tel: 028-9055 4422).

Just to the west of this is the late-1850s Italianate ★★★ **Sinclair Seamen's Presbyterian Church** ㉖, designed by Lanyon. Its interior owes more, however, to an optimist and imbiber, the Reverend Sam Cochrane R.N. The pitch-pine pulpit has the shape of a ship's prow flanked by navigation lights. The font is a ship's binnacle. A ship's bell calls lost souls to service. Collection boxes take the form of lifeboats. By the door a text reads 'A Merry Heart Doeth Good Like a Medicine'. Across the square stand both century-old sailortown bars and the ship's-timber-floored warehouse of **Direct Wine Shippers**.

*Maritime motifs in the Sinclair Seamen's church*

To the north of the Harbour Office, **Clarendon Road** leads into the newly redeveloped and attractive tree-lined riverside plazas surrounding ★★★ **Clarendon Dock** ㉗. The trees are ash and oak, the boulevards laid with stone paviours and square-setts, and many of the laid-up anchors and half-buried cannon bollards authentic. The 1862 Clarendon Building houses Laganside Corporation staff.

★ **Barrow Square** should be your next target. Its al-fresco entertainments include a month of world music every June marketed by FLAME (Festival at Lagan for Arts, Music and Education), which link in with the charms of adjoining the live-music oriented **Rotterdam** and **Pat's Bars** at the ends, respectively, of Pilot and Prince's Dock Streets. It is in the Rotterdam, that, allegedly, manacled prisoners were held before deportation to Van Diemen's Land (Tasmania).

Occasionally the evocative portside aromas of grain and flour waft waterwards as they are transported along Corporation Street. Carved symbols in the bright calm of **St Joseph's** Roman Catholic Church, built in 1880 in Prince's Dock Street, echo the maritime theme.

Across the Lagan, the huge yellow upturned Us of the cranes, called ★ **Samson and Goliath** by all but post-feminists who have rechristened the latter **Delilah**, dominate the eastern skyline over Queen's Island shipyards. Here Belfast men riveted the great metal skeleton that became the doomed *Titanic* in what were then the world's biggest shipyards. Access to the one-time offices of Andrews, Harland, Pirrie and Wolff is occasionally granted (tel. 028-9045 8456). Of late, the City Council has designated 15 April Titanic Day, and Harland & Wolff, cashing in on James Cameron's 1997 blockbuster movie, now licenses artefacts based on their copyright designs.

**35**

*Goliath*

Turning south, it's a windy walk through vanished docklands back past the sea-green glazing of the **Design Centre**, nearby which, at No. 18, David Allen's printworks was once the largest supplier of theatrical posters in the world. Nos. 1–7 Victoria Street were built as the Corn Exchange in 1851, Nos. 10–14 as shippers' insurers and Nos. 93–103 for a flour merchant.

While the Chapel of the Ford stood on the corner of High Street (left) from at least 1306, its ultimate successor, the high Anglican ★ **St George's** ㉘, dates from only 1813. Its classical portico was brought from the Earl Bishop of Derry's unfinished house. Perks for its first choirboys included all the salmon they could catch from the River Farset beyond the original wrought-iron rear gates. A plain memorial to Henry Pottinger (*see page 40*) is in tune with its plain interior. Opposite, on the Bank of Ireland – once the **National Bank –** octagonal fishscale turrets surmount a vigorous facade carved with centaurs and cornucopias.

The **McCausland Hotel**'s fine frontage is decorated with Thomas Fitzpatrick's ★ **splendid stonework** first devised for Lytle's and McCausland's Warehouses, Nos. 34–38 Victoria Street. For Lytle he carved frogs between waterlilies, squirrels stuffing with nuts, plus assorted birds and a pig-tailed Chinaman. For McCausland he presented the five trading continents in five robustly non-PC heads: Africa – an Ethiopian slave with broken chain and Nile lily; Asia – a Chinese girl in silks; Oceania – a South Sea Islander with coconuts; Europe – a self-satisfied be-whiskered Caucasian; North America – an indigenous 'Indian' complete with tomahawk and feather head-dress.

*Bittles' Bar*

*Kitchen Bar*

**Bittles' Bar**, packed with literary portraits, is tucked into the grid-iron shaped building at the corner of Victoria Street and otherwise ugly soulless Victoria Square. Yet this was once the theatrical heart of the city. Now the welcoming traditional 1859 stuccoed **Kitchen Bar** provides travellers in retreat from its brutal 1960s architecture with their only other solace.

Back, via Montgomery Street, on to Chichester (which locals pronounce Chai-Chester) Street, look east for a splendid vista of the Waterfront Hall, then west to the Black Mountain. The pleasant 1810-built **Garrick Bar** at No. 29 took its name from the fabled English thespian; its current customers ply other stages, the nearby Petty Sessions and Royal Courts of Justice.

Just west, Nos. 7–11 form an excellently restored terrace of four-storey Georgian houses in dusky red brick dating from 1804. They almost complete this route, which now proceeds across Donegall Square East from the red Ballachmoyle sandstone of Ocean Buildings, rich in exotic carvings of mermaids and monsters. For here, right in the corner of the City Hall grounds, there stands – ship's plans at hand – another reminder of Titanic Town: a Sicilian marble ★ **statue** of shipbuilder Sir Edward James Harland of Harland & Wolff.

# Route 4

*Inside the City Hall*

**North, to the Poorhouse**

**City Hall – conspirators' entries – historic banks – St Anne's Cathedral – Poorhouse – Courthouse – Gaol – Public Library – 1st Presbyterian Church – Donegall Place** *See map on page 14*

Route 4 runs north of the City Hall through the 'entries' (alleyways) that spawned the United Irishmen, to Poorhouse, Courthouse and Gaol.

*'Red brick on the gable/White Horse on the wall/Ital-i-an marble in the City Hall/Oh stranger from England, why look so aghast?/May the Lord in His Mercy look down on Belfast.'* Thus wrote poet-architect Maurice James Craig, deftly summarising the one-time ethos of this city of red-brick terraces and politico-historical folk art ruled with sectarian despatch from inside the marbled halls of Brumwell Thomas's 1906 wedding-cake ★★★ **City Hall** ❷⓽ (guided tours except public holidays October to May Monday to Saturday 2.30pm, Wednesday 11.30am; June to September Monday to Friday 10.30am, 11.30am, 2.30pm, Saturday 2.30pm; otherwise groups by arrangement, tel: 028-9032 0202 ext. 2346).

*The 'Wrenaissance' exterior*

The design, freely appropriated from St Paul's Cathedral in London, has been dubbed 'Wrenaissance'. A verdigrised copper Ionic dome rises to 53m (173ft) above the centre. Two storeys of a 100-m (33-ft) Portland stone quadrangle, each corner equipped with a tower, surround a central courtyard. In front stands Thomas Brock's statue of dumpy Queen Victoria, supported by a downtrodden but comely maiden spinning linen, a waif working material and a muscular shipwright's apprentice. Her back is to the

*The Great Dome*

*Among the statuary*

pedimented portico and its curious tomb-like porte-cochere, which suggests that Her Majesty, not amused, has stepped out of her mausoleum.

Further symbols of Edwardian arts and commerce, egged on by Hibernia and supported by Minerva and figures representing Industry, Labour and Liberty, are represented on the carved pediment, while inside an ornate Carrara marble staircase sweeps up from the Pavonazzo and Brescia marble grandiloquence of the Entrance Hall to the Rotunda colonnaded in Cippalino marble. Off this are Reception Room, Banqueting Hall and wainscotted Council Chamber laid out on the Westminster House of Commons model. Above the Rotunda, under the Great Dome, is the **whispering gallery** and John Luke's mural of the city's industries.

Outside, a further series of statues punctuates the lawns, commemorating worthies, from frock-coated mayors to James Magennis who gained his Victoria Cross in World War II placing mines from a midget submarine well behind enemy lines. It took over 50 years for Unionist councillors to commemorate this ill-educated Catholic hero.

Just as telling is the bronze statue of the **Marquess of Dufferin and Ava**, portrayed as a moustached and breeches-clad imperial temple deity, chest out under a canopy topped by a winged goddess and surrounded by his servants, a turbanned sabre-toting Sikh warrior astride a cannon and, on a dead moose, a Canadian trapper complete with pelts and snow-shoes. Thus saluted are his achievements as Viceroy of India and Governor-General of Canada. No mention here of his involvement in Stock Exchange scandals which led to another's suicide.

Where, in November 1995, US President Bill Clinton addressed huge crowds celebrating a possible cessation of terrorism, a single column of Portland stone effectively recalls the first European touch-down of the **US Expeditionary Force** who disembarked in Belfast on 26 January 1942. Another sober restrained monument serves as the World War I and World War II Cenotaph on Remembrance Sunday. It, too, was designed by Brumwell Thomas, who had to sue the City Fathers for his fees.

Across **Donegall Square North**, turning right from the City Hall gates, the influence of Lanyon's firm crops up again in the red sandstone four-storey Venetian Gothic mass, completed in 1869 as a linen warehouse. This later became the Water Office until magisterially restored by ★ **Marks & Spencer**, the carved vegetable frieze quite suiting their business. On New Year's Day 1884, Oscar Wilde proclaimed this the city's sole beautiful building.

Taking its name from callendering, a smoothing process for linen, **Callender Street** was once an alleyway for the

*Marks & Spencer*

complimentary businesses of distilling and newspaper publishing, now a short-cut through to pedestrianised **Castle Lane** with its centuries-old flower market. To the right, five streets converge on **Arthur Square** with its spindly red bandstand clock tower, a favourite with the city's obsessively bellowing evangelists. There is fine Art Nouveau detailing on the 1906 Mayfair Building. The 1870 ★ **Masonic Building**, Nos. 13–21, is by Lanyon's firm and stands on the site of oyster taverns, a trade that prospered down William Street South. Here in 1875, from still attractive Nos. 13–19, William Ross planned wells 130m (420ft) deep to obtain pure water for his still extant and celebrated Belfast Ginger Ale. Centuries back, Donegalls moored their pleasure barges in what is now Arthur Street, and the Corn Market was what it says it was.

*Castle Lane paving*

In **Ann Street**, straight ahead, none of several once-thriving theatres survive, but its other business, boot-making, continues through a number of cut-price shoe shops which match the tone of today's thoroughfare.

*Ann Street*

Before his execution, the 1798 Presbyterian leader Henry Joy McCracken was held in No. 13 when it served as the Artillery Barracks, before being hanged in the Corn Market. However, our interest lies in nipping in and out of the quarter's narrow pub-lined entries. From **Joy's Entry** in 1737 the Revolutionary martyr's grandfather Francis Joy established what is now the oldest continuously published newspaper in the English language, the *Belfast News Letter*. The predecessor to its current rival, the *Irish News*, developed from the *Morning News*, first published in 1853 at No. 6 **Crown Entry**. The Society of United Irishmen was inaugurated in the Crown Tavern in 1791. Absurdly indiscreet, and fond of a jar, they were betrayed by 'Belle Martin, a buxom barmaid working Peggy Barclay's other tavern, Dr Franklin's (a.k.a. The Muddlers' Club), then in skimpiest entry of all, **Sugar-house Entry**, running from High Street to Waring Street.

From **Wilson's Court** the first edition of the United Irishmen's own newspaper, the *Northern Star*, was published, and Belfast playwright Stewart Parker's play of the same name takes a sardonically sympathetic view of their editorial meetings. **Hamilton's Court** housed an 18th-century town sovereign. Born in a humble cooper's house in Cole's Entry, actress and courtesan Harriet Mellon rose to become Duchess of St Albans. The acclaimed landscape watercolourist and printmaker Andrew Nicholl (1804–86) was a bootmaker's son from **Church Lane**, where among the 18th and 19th-century houses **The Glass Jar** (once his studio) claims to be Belfast's narrowest bar.

*The Glass Jar, Belfast's narrowest bar*

This route, however, ducks under a painted brick archway into **Pottinger's Entry**, past the distracting ambience of the ornate **Morning Star** where Mary McCracken attempted to revive her brother, having first bribed the hangman. It is the last of the area's celebrated oyster houses. The cut is named after the Pottinger family who supplied the city with sovereigns and the British army with moustached majors. The most noted of the family was Henry, who as Governor secured the British lease to Hong Kong after the Chinese Opium Wars.

**High Street** takes the line of the Farset river which still flows beneath it. Here lived the McCracken family and Sir James Murray, patentor of Milk of Magnesia. To the left are St George's Buildings, three storeys of attractively detailed stucco, behind which the city's first cinema opened in the Central Hall on 17 August 1908, packing 1,500 in for a showing of the silent movie *Bluebeard*.

**Skipper Street** provided lodging for tea clipper skippers. **Waring Street**, beyond, is named after William Waring, a tanner whose house was at No. 30, where Benny Conlon's, a tiny newshound's bar, preserves its and his anonymity. His daughter, Jane, grew up to become Dean Jonathan Swift's *Varina*, refusing him marriage while he was prebendary at Kilroot, near Carrickfergus, in 1696.

*Ulster Bank*

Opposite Jane's place of birth stand first, on the corner, the 1869 solid sandstone block named the Ulster Buildings, then the 1860 ★ **Ulster Bank** ㉚ with its elaborate cast-iron balustrade and extravaganza of Thomas Fitzpatrick's carvings. The skyline is dominated by his

*Britannia, Justice and Commerce*

★★ **figures** of Britannia, Justice and Commerce. Urns surmount the corners. The interior is equally fascinating, sporting an octagonally based dome and figures representing Music, Poetry, Science and Sculpture.

The **Northern Ireland War Memorial Building** (Monday to Friday 9am–5pm, free), at Nos. 9–13, includes a Hall of Friendship and the Museum of the Royal Ulster Rifles and their predecessor, foot regiments first raised in 1793.

At the opposite end of the street, across what was once the Four Corners at the entrance to Donegall Street, is another excellent building, the original 1769 ★ **Exchange** converted to a bank, the Northern, by Lanyon in 1845. Italianate stucco, the architect's trademark, is everywhere. All mileage from Belfast was calculated from here and in 1792 the premises hosted the famous Harp Festival, during which the young musicologist Edward Bunting transcribed the traditional airs and compositions of the last of this island's blind harpers. Opposite, the grey 1819 Dublin granite bulk of the **Commercial Buildings** with their Ionic pillars and Doric porches housed first a cotton warehouse and more recently the *Northern Whig* newspaper.

Paved with setts and with its many hidden courtyards, entries (their corners protected from carriage wheels by heavy iron bollards) and listed brick and stucco ware-houses, **Hill Street** is catalyst for the city's latest regeneration area, modelled it is said with some facility, on Dublin's Temple Bar. Perhaps it is also due to the presence of the Historic Monuments and Buildings Branch of the Department of the Environment at Nos. 5–33.

Exchange Place houses the avant-garde and airy spaces of the **Catalyst Arts** cooperative. The Duke of York in Commercial Court was a hacks' pub where Gerry Adams, leader of Sinn Féin, worked as a barman in the 1960s.

A left turn leads to largely demolished Talbot Street running alongside the Protestant ★ **Cathedral ㉛**, a neo-Romanesque construction of Portland stone begun in 1898 and still lacking a spire. It succeeds a previous Parish Church, named as much after Anne, wife of the fifth Earl of Donegall, as Mary's mother. The current rather plain nave's spaciousness is due in part to it being built around its predecessor, where services were held until 1903. The pulpit, designed by Gilbert Scott, was carved by Harry Hems. The other curiosity is why it was built at all, for the diocese of Down, Connor and Dromore already had three cathedrals. The burghers of Belfast, however, said Belfast was not a proper city without a bishop's throne (cathedra).

**41**

High up on the old painted sandstone chateauesque former offices of the Unionist *News Letter*, right on Donegall Street at Nos. 49–67, are the carved heads of literary lions. Other architectural entertainments on the old linen warehouses are all above eye level, including the Celtic capitals over No. 3. Otherwise, this is the bleak end of a bleak street, described thus by William Drennan back in 1796. An artists' movement works from an old linen museum, now Paragon Studios at No. 18 and an excellent diversion is **North Street Arcade**, a 1930s shopping

*North Street Arcade*
*The Cathedral*

mall housing the adventurous **Proposition Gallery** and artists' studios.

Opposite the Cathedral, the relaxing predictability of the urban parkland is relieved by diverting sculptural pieces by John Kindness and Brian Connolly whose globe, literally, needs looking into. Sadly, neither sculptor nor the ★★ **N.I. Tourist Board** ㉜, whose offices overlook the park, make reference to The Monkey Shaving The Goat, a tavern once here before the streets were cleared away.

Right off Donegall Street is **Academy Street**, so called after David Manson's 1768 co-educational establishment. Despite regulations forbidding dogs and guns, nine pupils at No. 2, now demolished but once the Belfast Academy, took their masters hostage at gunpoint when they heard Easter Holidays were to be cancelled. No. 40, built as a distiller's warehouse, now houses the Belfast Education and Library Board. Across from the pleasing facade of the 1901 Cathedral Buildings, harbour buoys decorate a park space outside the Ulster University's ghastly Art School.

*Harbour buoys, Cathedral Buildings in the background*

Back on Donegall Street, across the top of **Royal Avenue**, is another journalist's pub with the giveaway name of The Front Page, opposite the **Irish News** (the Catholic morning paper). The adjoining frontage is a pleasant 1932 reconstruction of the German blitz-damaged 1860 sandstone of **Donegall Street Congregational Church**.

*Irish News premises*

John Willis, first organist at the Gothic Revivalist **St Patrick's** Roman Catholic Church beyond, was dismissed almost as soon as he was engaged for playing variations on *The Boyne Water*, a belligerent Orange Protestant marching tune, at a service. The murky side chapel triptych of St Patrick, the Madonna and St Bridget is by the society painter and war artist Sir John Lavery. The elegant three-storey houses north, from 1796 or 1820, have recently been restored, making them, either way, among the earliest block of domestic premises to survive in the city.

*St Patrick at his church*

The crossing of Carrick Hill, a haunt of pimps and rent boys in the 1850s, though still perilous for the pedestrian, is worthwhile. The Poorhouse, now ★★ **Clifton House** ㉝, though much altered, is still one of the most delightfully modest public Georgian buildings in Ireland. A central two-storey red-brick block is flanked by single-storey wings with gabled end pavilions and its octagonal central tower forms a pleasing focal point. In still spacious grounds donated by Lord Donegall, to designs prepared by Robert Joy (then editor of the *Belfast News Letter*), it opened in 1774, housing (as it still does) the poor and indigent, hosting grand balls to pay for their upkeep.

Followers of Route 4 can turn back here, heading for Royal Avenue with no disgrace, but Lanyon aficionados will soldier on north up Clifton Street, under the unbending gaze of Harry Hems' striking 3-m (10-ft) 3-ton life-sized bronze of ★ **King Billy**, sabre drawn, the city's sole equestrian monument on the roof of **Clifton Street Orange Hall**. Mary Ann, Henry Joy McCracken's feisty feminist sister, is buried in the Clifton Street **burial ground**, near (probably) her heroic brother. Also under the sod here lies the man who coined the phrase 'Emerald Isle', Dr William Drennan, another founder member of the United Irishman.

North past **Carlisle Circus** are Lanyon's deliberately sinister Piranesian ★ **Gaol** and his formidable Corinthian ★★ **Crown Courthouse** ㉞, their peacetime futures uncertain, facing each other across, and joined by a tunnel below, the Crumlin Road. A further Lanyon delight, **St Paul's** Church of Ireland, can be found by enthusiasts, improving the view from the unlovely Yorkgate train station on York Street. Further up is the **Flax International Arts Centre's** Golden Thread Dance Studio, Gallery and Theater Plus.

Coming back into the city, the **Belfast Telegraph**, a liberal-minded evening paper with but a lower-case 'u' to its Unionist stance, stands on the corner of Donegall Street and Royal Avenue, which has been the city's main shopping thoroughfare since Victorian times. The *'Tele's'* much-altered red-brick and red Dumfries sandstone building dates, as does much of the avenue, from the mid-1880s. Despite IRA bombs and thoughtless shopfronts, much of the original survives in the ornamental brick and rich zoomorphically carved stucco above ground-floor level.

Next to the newspaper is the French-looking three-storey **Belfast Public Library**, also in red sandstone, designed by Lanyon's partner Lynn and completed in 1888. Lynn also simultaneously devised the gentlemen's Reform Club at No. 4 while the Portland stone Art Deco Bank of Ireland, with its relief-carved stylised female head, was erected 50 years later. The Northern Bank at Nos. 109–111 is by John Lanyon, Charles' son, and ★ **Provincial Bank** (now a Tesco Metro) at No. 2 by their rival W.J. Barrie.

*Belfast Public Library*

Progressing towards Donegall Place and City Hall, the Albert, Gresham and Crown Chambers, on the right, retain some of their period charm, as do Donegall, Eagle, Royal and Avenue Chambers on the left. The reflective glass and stainless steel of **Castlecourt** shopping mall, was, when it arrived in 1985, hailed for the confidence of its investors in a city not yet, despite decades of commercial conflagration, turned to peaceful ways. Until the 1960s this had been the Grand Central Hotel, boasting Al Jolson, John McCormack and Paul Robeson among its guests. Later it housed the British Army's colonels and squaddies, spies and double agents.

*Royal Avenue*

However, Route 4 diverts east into **Rosemary Street** where Sarah Siddons, the celebrated actress, played its long-gone 18th-century Playhouse just opposite the truly delightful ★★ First (Non-Subscribing) **Presbyterian Church** ㉟. Dating from 1781, this is the city's oldest surviving place of worship. Its interior is boat-like and elliptical, its woodwork divine, its ceiling radially plastered, its pews boxed, its lunchtime concerts oases in this modest metropolis. Such was the fervour of dogma among 18th-century Dissenters that splits led them to build two further separate churches, since demolished, in the same street. A pity, for the United Irishmen plotted in the loft of the Second. William Drennan, a leading United Irishman, was born in the building which, then the manse, stood to the left. It had been built for the Rev Robert McBride, from whom Edgar Alan Poe was descended.

The route turns right into **Lombard Street**, from which the Irish Temperance League once operated, then smartly left again into the courtyard of **Winecellar Entry**, past the upturned cannon-barrel bollards to **White's Tavern**, associated with the wine trade since 1630 but rebuilt many many times. A further right turn in this dingy canyon returns the traveller on to High Street opposite Pottinger's Entry. Here the route continues left up High Street past the splendid Art Deco bulk of what was a 1930s Woolworth's and Burton's department store, standing on the site of the Market House from which, during the 1798 rebellion, corpses were hung out to rot.

Little remains in **Castle Place** that would suggest its former Victorian commercial focus as a place of silk mercers and tea shops and indeed of previous glories. The street furniture is ubiquitous and where Donegal Arcade now runs was once the Provost Prison where those to be hanged from the Market House were held. Lanyon's Ulster Club of No. 23 is long gone. However, W. H. Lynn's

*Kelly's Cellars (above) and White's Tavern*

five-storey red sandstone Bank Buildings, now Primark, the Victorian and Art Nouveau detail high up on the Woolwich at No. 17 and Castle Buildings at Nos. 8–18, do give a flavour of past times and glory.

Just right of the old Bank Buildings, **Bank Street** runs west to **Kelly's Cellars**, a public house established in 1720 and even today retaining some of the conspiratorial ambience generated when Henry Joy McCracken crouched beneath the counter escaping the Redcoats. A left turn takes us into **Chapel Lane**, past St Mary's Roman Catholic Chapel, whose walls date from 1783 and whose original opening was formally and ecumenically saluted by the Presbyterians of the 1st Belfast Volunteer Company.

Scruffy with black taxis and fruit and vegetable stalls, **Castle Street** is home to the 1865 Hercules Bar, the Irish Tourist Board (a.k.a. Bord Fáilte) and Aer Lingus, the Irish national airline. British Airways is based in College Street, off Fountain Street, from which the 1880s-built Queen's Arcade leads back on to **Donegall Place**.

Though colonised almost entirely by British high-street multiples, the Place does, as usual in its upper storeys, reflect its former vernacular confidence. Above **Queen's Arcade Buildings** is a Disneyesque maquette of Belfast Castle. Habitat occupies an 1895 beige sandstone rich in carved portraits real and mythological. The stucco edifice next door dates from 20 years earlier. Nos. 36–38 retain, on the second floor, the legend *Tempus Fugit* plus Father Time with hour-glass and scythe, attesting to its origins as a clockmakers'. The cartouche reading a century earlier refers misleadingly to the original owner's grandfather. No. 25 is in essence a 200-year-old house, which, when it was a fur shop, sold garments 'sufficient to tempt a lady to break the 10th commandment'. Charles Dickens lodged in the hotel that stood at the left-hand corner with Donegall Square North. Thackeray had rooms here too, declaring them 'as comfortable and well-ordered an establishment as the most fastidious Cockney can desire'.

*Queen's Arcade Buildings and Habitat detail*

**45**

Across the Place stands what was once the province's leading store, still bearing the name, high up, of **Robinson & Cleaver's**. Originally a linen warehouse it has six storeys, a clock tower, ogee copper domes and, carved by Harry Hems, a flock of Donatello cherubs and 50 stone heads of those claimed as the firm's patrons, plus symbolic references to far-flung marketplaces. Thus Queen Victoria, Prince Albert, George Washington and the man who first delineated the rules of snooker, the Maharaja of Cooch Behar, as well as Australia and Canada are easily identified. Now a McDonald's trades on street level, as one colonial imperative replaces another. *Sic transit gloria* perhaps, but Queen Victoria stands sturdy as ever across Donegall Square North.

*Robinson & Cleaver's*

*View up the coast from Cave Hill*

# Route 5

Napoleon's Nose

## Cave Hill Country Park – Belfast Castle – McArt's Fort – Cave Hill – Hazelwood – Zoo

This route walks the Cave Hill, giving an overview of the city sprawling down below, exploring rugged baronial Castle, forest, nature reserve and zoo.

Looking west, north or east from almost anywhere in Belfast you can see that the city is cupped in a saucer of hills. Clockwise from the west they are the **Black Mountain**, **Cave Hill**, the **Castlereagh Hills** and the drumlins of County Down, all framed at the ends of the shallow canyons of the streets. Most spectacular is the profile of ★★ **Cave Hill** , 'Napoleon's Nose' to locals, seen from Fisherwick Place, looking north. Even more satisfying than the view, though, is the 6-km (4-mile) climb up the hill to look down on the Lagan estuary with the sprawl of Belfast (*Béal Feirste,* the approach to the sandbank ford, as it was originally called in Irish) for miles below.

CityBuses Nos 2–6, 8–10 and 45 run the distance up the **Antrim Road** with a stop at suburban **Strathmore Park** from where the climb begins, first past the castle's isolated turreted former **Gatelodge**, designed by Charles Lanyon's son, John. Then uphill and right along **Downview Park West** with the castle's Gothic former **mortuary chapel**, built to drawings by the Lanyons' partner W. H. Lynn to the right in Innisfayle Park.

A left turn brings us into ★ **Belfast Castle Estate** and up to the ★★ **Castle** ③⑦, a ruggedly ro-

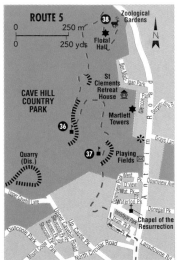

**ROUTE 5**

0 ⎯⎯⎯ 250 m
0 ⎯⎯⎯ 250 yds

**Zoological Gardens** ③⑧

Floral Hall

CAVE HILL COUNTRY PARK

St Clements Retreat House

Ben Madigan

Logan Park

Glencairn Rd

Serpentine Park

Martlett Towers

Grays Lan

③⑥

③⑦

Playing Fields

Quarry (Dis.)

West Pk

Downview Ave

Upper Cavehill Lane

D'view

Wat. Pk

Waterloo Pk

Donegall Pk

Chapel of the Resurrection

Duncoole Park

Upper Cavehill Road

Strand Pk

Lin Castle Rd

Shancoole Park

Shancoole Pk

North Circular Road

Lansdowne Rd

mantic Scots baronial pile rich in turrets and faced with Cookstown sandstone. It was constructed in 1865 for the impoverished 3rd marquis of Donegall, again by Charles Lanyon's son John, who borrowed freely from Prince Albert's sketches for his recently completed Balmoral Castle. Lanyon Jnr.'s fees were guaranteed by the marquis's daughter, Harriet, who had taken the precaution of marrying the immensely rich 8th earl of Shaftesbury. Their son, the 9th earl, presented the castle to the Corporation in 1934.

Walkers should call in at the useful **Cavehill Heritage Centre** for detailed maps. There is a series of restaurants and wedding photographers take advantage of the sensuous curves of an engorged and serpentine protruding exterior **staircase** connecting *piano nobile* to garden terrace below.

*Belfast Castle and Gardens*

However, the Cave Hill walk proper through the 200-acre estate begins in the car park a bit further downhill, climbing on gravelled paths up to a T-junction where the correct direction is right, giving a view of the castle below as you continue through the woods, taking main turns left, then upward. Out from the woods a steeper path takes a left right up to the mouth of the titular **cave** first used by Neolithic hunter-gatherers. Just before the cave-mouth, a further left runs even more steeply towards what looks like a notch in the skyline but which is in fact a defensive ditch to ★ **Mc Art's Fort** on the 400-m (1,180-ft) high promontory. This is alternatively referred to as **Napoleon's Nose** or **Ben Madigan** (from *beann*, the Irish for peak) after a 9th-century King of Ulster.

Foxes trail rabbits through heather. Kestrel and peregrine hover and stoop. Badgers wander at night through the Maytime bluebells. Yet Belfast sprawls before you, a mite different from the days when the Neolithic hunters (whose raths dot the slopes) hoped to liberate all they surveyed, followed later by Cormac McAirt, then Henry Joy McCracken. This is also where, in May 1795, Wolfe Tone, a Protestant coachbuilder's son, and his United Irishmen took their solemn oath of *liberté, égalité, fraternité.* Romantic revolutionaries meet here in annual commemoration of Tone's capture in 1798.

The route continues due north towards (but not too near) the cliff's edge, before descending alongside a stream through **Hazelwood Nature Reserve**. This brings you on to a better path, then steps, to the perimeter of the **Zoo** ㊳, whose entrance is to the left (April to September, 10am 5pm daily; October to March, Saturday to Thursday 10am–3.30pm, Friday till 2.30pm). Though the *Ah-Zoo* as, it is locally pronounced, has an admirable captive breeding programme for rare animals, you may prefer to turn right along its perimeter uphill into open country. Cave Hill soars above, with the castle straight ahead.

*The rare lion-tailed macaque, Belfast Zoo*

*Falls Road Park*

## Route 6

**Troubled Times**

Castle Place – Royal Avenue – Donegall Quay – Queen
Elizabeth Bridge – Short Strand – Newtownards Road
– Ormeau Road – Queen's University – Sandy Row
– The Falls – Shankill – Crumlin Road *See maps on
page 14 and right*

This route tours areas of the city made notorious in 30 years
of civic unrest.

Belfast's sectarian riots didn't just begin when the IRA
intensified its 'armed struggle' in 1969–70. Since its foundation, the city has had a history of Catholic against Protestant, and Dissenter against established church. Many city-
centre buildings were fire-bombed in the 1970s and 1980s
but the war of attrition was fought in outlying east and west
Belfast – too far on foot for any but dedicated activist, war
historian or conflict zone groupie.

*Loyalist mural*
*Nationalist mural*

Here the dominant landscape can be a bleak mix of
abandoned linen mills, pristine public parks, burnt-out
shops, secured shopping malls, empty lots, churches,
gable-end murals promoting the cause of the dozens of
paramilitary factions. Police stations became fortresses.
British Army bases went, literally, underground. Or they
set themselves up atop populated tower blocks reckon-
ing the proximity of ordinary citizens offered protection
while their sophisticated electronics eavesdropped on even
the whispered sweet nothings of terrorist suspects.

But look again. Most houses are new, well-made
products of a Herculean exemplary effort in public re-
housing, instituted over those decades of ethnic cleansing,

by the admirably impartial Northern Ireland Housing Executive which now markets its expertise to the crumbling remnants of the Soviet empire. Factories are turned into enterprise parks firmly committed to a cross-community ethos. New academic campuses are planned.

Thus there is a fascination in taking CityBus's **Belfast: A Living History** tour (*see page 74*), which ducks few difficult questions and remains, in route and commentary, as impartial as the Housing Executive whose estates it passes. Or you can follow the route by car, cycle or taxi.

Henry Joy McCracken, Presbyterian hero of the failed 1798 rebellion, was hanged that year in the **Cornmarket** off **Castle Place** ❸❾ where this route begins. Much of **Bridge Street** was devastated by the 1941 German air raids. **Donegall Street**, home until lately to the Protestant-oriented newspaper, the *News Letter,* leads to **Royal Avenue**, site of Hercules Lane meat market where the cobbles ran red with Catholic and Protestant blood when butchers from both sides of the divide clashed in 1864.

*Former 'News Letter' facade*

Turning left at **City Hall** (*see page 37*), proceed down **Chichester Street** whose new buildings grew out of IRA devastation. Along **Victoria Street** meetings by the **Custom House** (*see page 33*) on **Donegall Quay** during the dock strike of 1907 made this Belfast's Speakers' Corner until terrorism made such public expression inadvisable.

The naming of **Queen Elizabeth Bridge** in 1967 throws further light on a divided city, Unionists insisting on

*Queen Elizabeth Bridge*

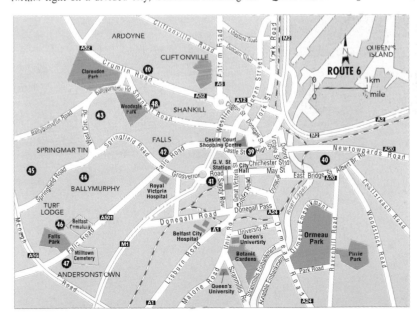

*Harland & Wolff shipyard*

*UVF mural*

*Ormeau Bridge*

calling it after their hero Sir Edward Carson until forced by the Queen's government to accept a name marginally less unpalatable to Nationalists and Republicans.

From 1889 onwards at Queen's Island, Harland & Wolff established, with the *Oceanic*, their tradition of building the world's largest ships. But sectarian riots, explored in Sam Thompson's seminal play *Over The Bridge*, were as much a factor of a shipworker's life as riveting.

A quiet security force 'peaceline' of brick and shrubbery surrounding the tiny Catholic enclave of **Short Strand ④** stands evidence to the history of this locality's inter-Christian brutalities. In turn UVF (Ulster Volunteer Force), UDA (Ulster Defence Association), LPA (Loyalist Prisoners Army), UFF (Ulster Freedom Fighters), UPD (Ulster Past Defenders), UYM (Ulster Young Militants) murals depict balaclaved men carrying AK47 assault rifles, proclaiming a steadfast 'No Surrender'. Cuchullain, Hound of Ulster, the warrior hero of the Red Branch knights at Ard Macha (now the city of Armagh, Ulster's Camelot), is another icon. The Royal Shakespeare Company has played the **Tower Street Theatre**, and the **Engine Room** is a thriving contemporary art gallery.

Back through **Templemore Avenue** across the Lagan by the **Albert Bridge** and your bus is in the **Cromac Street Markets** area, another Catholic enclave in the east of the city. Here residents clashed with Dr Ian Paisley's Democratic Unionists in 1966. Further south, past the gentrified **Gasworks** at **Ormeau Bridge**, police maintain an uneasy human peaceline each summer between Catholic Republican residents and Protestant Orangemen from south of the river. Here graffiti has a sardonic wit lacking elsewhere: a bowler-hatted Orangeman on a no-entry traffic sign.

Along University Street and Road, past **Queen's University** (*see page 25*) where the civil rights marches of 1968 were planned, the route turns along the **Lisburn Road** into another Orange heartland, **Sandy Row ④**, beyond which Protestant linen spinners clashed with Catholic cotton weavers north of the **Boyne Bridge** through the 19th century. Beyond **Durham Street** and **College Square North** at **Millfield** 'black taxis' declare Republican allegiance, naming destinations in both English and Irish.

Many high-rise, low-income tower blocks have been demolished, but the **Lower Falls ④** still displays many icons illustrating passions that tore the area apart. Divis Tower is still called *Planet of the IRSPs* (Irish Republican Socialist Party). A Madonna and Child on the **Springfield Road** dignifies the gable of Brickfield, the city's first purpose-built police station. At Sevastapol Street, and thence uphill, the memorial murals are for Bobby Sands, later Bobby Sands, the MP who was the first of the 10 Republican hunger-strikers to die after a 66-day fast in

1981. Stark peaceline walls and mobile security barriers separate conclaves and a green oasis, **Dunville Park**, is named after its whiskey-distilling benefactor.

The names of the housing estates are roll calls of 30 years of terror's headlines: **Springmartin** ⓭, **Ballymurphy** ⓮, **New Barnsley**, **Whiterock** ⓯ – where the British Army took their barracks underground, but also where the thriving DubbelJoint (Dub for Dublin/Bel for Belfast) Theatre Company premiers its challenging repertoire – **Turf Lodge** ⓰ and **Andersonstown** ⓱. Old men and small boys trotting greyhounds smile at the tourists. Women smoke on the street. Tougher-looking citizens don't return a wave. But Bass brews fine Caffrey's Ale on the **Glen Road**. Gypsies have gained squatters rights on bends of the road. Off Shaw's Road **Rossgoill** is a Gaelic-speaking cantonment.

Back on the **Falls** are Sinn Féin Headquarters; the Felons' Club and murals for the heroes of the 1916 Rising in Dublin. **Milltown Cemetery** is where on live television loyalist paramilitary Michael Stone shot and threw grenades at mourners at a Republican funeral. Celtic Park is where Winston Churchill spoke to the Home Rulers in 1912. Few Protestants bury their dead in the City Cemetery which Catholics once shunned. St Louise's is the largest girls' school in western Europe and the **Royal Victoria Hospital** now leads the world in war trauma treatment. On **Peter's Hill** the eponymous pro-Cathedral's twin spires lined up the sights of World War II German bombers.

*Commemorating the 1916 Rising*

**51**

Head north up the run-down Protestant **Shankill** ⓲, its houses and shops gone, its memorial murals faded, its ageing population worshipping at the shamrock-shaped 1872 St Matthew's Church of Ireland.

At the apex of Woodvale and **Crumlin Road** ⓳, the peaceline marks off Catholic Ardoyne, beside where 20,000 were employed in the once-great linen mills now silent, only Flax and Cambrai Streets reminding us of their raw material, flax grown from seed imported from the Belgian town of Cambrai. Until the 1930s schoolkids followed four hours in the mills with four tired hours in school, trapping themselves, ill educated, into a short, unhealthy linen lifetime while crowned heads and robber barons spilled claret on the hard-wrought damask.

*The peaceline wall*

South, downhill, a county courthouse and a house of correction, both Lanyon designs, awaited those uncomfortable with such a division of the spoils of labour. And what's beyond for you? If you head past **Carlisle Circus** and its Troubles-wasted acres, you come upon the New Burying Ground (where you might rot beside Henry Joy McCracken after a stay in the poorhouse), then **Clifton House**, the city's chaste and finest 18th-century building).

# Riverside Walks

For those who want a pleasant walk near the heart of the city, nowhere is better than to follow the circular **Riverside Walkway** upstream to Ormeau Bridge. The vernacular riverine streetscape has been re-profiled, evoking pleasant mythic quayside pasts. Starting at **Lagan Weir** the walkway heads south past the two Queen's Bridges and along the left bank skirting Waterfront Hall, a Hilton and the BT building to a riverside pub at May's Meadow. From there it crosses East Bridge Street to St George's Harbour and continues past the Gasworks regeneration and Haulier's Walk to Ormeau Bridge. It continues across the bridge and back downstream along the **Ormeau Embankment** (with pleasant Ormeau Park on the right) to Ravenhill Reach, losing the river along Ravenhill Road, but rejoining it at Pottinger's Quay. Then come Laganview and Gregg's Quay, and to the north of the Queen's Bridges **Abercorn Basin**, whose attractions include the Millennium Odyssey 13,000-seat arena, Science Centre and IMAX theatre, plus **Titanic Park** on Queen's Island.

*Crossing Lagan Weir*

**52**

*Along the Towpath*

It is also possible to explore the wooded parkland off the **Lagan Towpath** further upstream. Here, linen barons' mansions recall the Lagan Canal's part in a grandiose 19th-century scheme to create an inland Belfast to Dublin water route. Walks begin on Lockview Road, alfresco, at **Cutter's Wharf**'s pub quay, reached by the No 69 Stranmillis CityBus. There is a free car park beyond with maps prominently displayed on noticeboards. The path descends through wildflower grasslands, into the Ulster Wildlife Trust's **Lagan Valley Nature Reserve** and across the Lagan Canal. Another footbridge, across the River Lagan, leads into **Belvoir** (pronounced beaver) **Forest Park**. Otherwise follow the left bank of the Lagan downstream, crossing a wooded island between canal and river. A footbridge crosses the canal, leading back to Cutter's Wharf.

Left-bank explorers can continue upstream by **Clement Wilson Park**, and past the 1709 **Shaw's Bridge** where the No 13 UlsterBus stops. From here there's a possible diversion to **Barnett's Demense** with its elegant 1820s house, restaurant and art gallery (where the No 71 CityBus stops). Another 10 km (6 miles) takes in **Sir Thomas and Lady Dixon Park** with its mansion and magnificent rolling acres. Following the right bank upstream a 6-km (4-mile) loop takes the walker past the linen village of **Edenderry** to the **Giant's Ring** dolmen and back by road.

*The Giant's Ring*

True walkers taking the five-hour towpath walk to Lisburn's **Irish Linen Centre** (*see page 56*) should remember there are no cafés, pubs or shops along the way bar **Hilden's micro-brewery**. Trains and buses back to Belfast are frequent, though, with stops usually near bridges.

# Excursion 1

*High summer on the coast*

### Gold Coast, Viking Lough

The north Down coast bears with some pride its tabloid
sobriquet, the Gold Coast. Indeed there is, in the bosky
avenues around the pretty English-style commuter villages
of Holywood, Crawfordsburn and Helen's Bay, enough
conspicuous wealth to support the illusion that this is the
fiefdom of high-flying barristers and civil servants.

The ★ **Old Inn** at **Crawfordsburn**, amid the Crawfordsburn Country Park, claims to be Ireland's oldest
(1614) coaching inn, an ideal place to round off a visit
to the panoramas of Ulster's vernacular past displayed
in the rolling acres of ★★★ **Ulster Folk and Transport
Museum** (April to June, Monday to Friday 9am–5pm,
weekends 10–6pm; July to September, 10am–6pm daily;
October to March, 9am–4pm daily) Here are whole terraces of 19th century houses moved stone by stone to their
new address, plus schools, thatched cottages and a rectory.

*The Old Inn at Crawfordsburn*

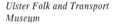

*Ulster Folk and Transport
Museum*

Here too you learn a secret language. Ulster's citizens
describe one of another Christian faith as 'digging with
the other foot'. At the working forge you learn that in the
days before good roads, townlands were isolated and thus
the turf spade (*loy*) designed for the land of one village
might not suit another soil. Since each settlement tended
to be of a single religion, a stranger became one who 'dug
with the other foot'. Across the road, in the transport
section, steam and aircraft buffs will be in their element.

From the dormitory and marina town of ★ **Bangor** with
its **North Down Heritage Centre** (Tuesday to Saturday
10.30am–4.30pm, Sunday 2–4.30pm; to 5.30pm in July and
August), and from quaint Groomsport and busy **Donaghadee** there are trips (summer only) to the bird-rich
★ **Copeland Islands**. Keats, Wordsworth and Daniel

*Ballycopeland Windmill*

Defoe landed at the 'Dee, on spying missions for the English Crown. The composer Franz Liszt came, complete with his piano. And Peter the Great, buying horses. ★ **Grace Neill's Bar** in Donaghadee's High Street, dating from 1611, claims to have dined them all. The **lighthouse**, designed by Sir John Rennie who built the Eddystone Light off Plymouth, hired the future playwright Brendan Behan as a house painter. The mound off Moat Street was once a gunpowder store. ★★ **Ballycopeland Windmill** (closed Sunday morning, Monday, and October to March) is a relief from Millisle's caravan-covered acres.

Along the **Ards Peninsula**'s eastern shores seals bob in the fishing harbour of **Portavogie** and terns dip and Manx shearwaters cry against the wind, skimming the waves at rocky **Kearney**, a clachan (small village) preserved by the National Trust. From its western shores, in effect the eastern shores of the inlet of ★★★ **Strangford Lough**, you can watch hundreds of thousands of migratory waders among the pladdies, tiny islands of gravel left behind as the Ice Age retreated. Many of the 2,000-plus marine creatures the waders feed on, plus other larger lough dwellers, are well displayed in ★★ **Exploris Aquarium** in **Portaferry** (Monday to Friday 10am–5pm, Saturday 11am–5pm, Sunday 1–5pm). ★ **Portaferry Hotel** has one of the best seafood kitchens in the country.

Up the western shore, a physick garden adds to the charm of the late 12th-century Cistercian ★★ **abbey ruins** at **Greyabbey**, while strange topiary and anthropomorphic statuary sugar the appeal of the National Trust's 18th-century ★★★ **Mount Stewart** (house and grounds open daily April to September, 11.30am–5pm; October to March, weekends 11.30am–5.30pm; Tuesday grounds only open). Inside, George Stubbs's portrait of the racehorse Hambletonian is the province's best painting.

A dawn-to-dusk ★★ **ferry** carries cars across the swirling waters to **Strangford**, with its defensive towerhouse and the National Trust-owned ★★★ **Castle Ward** (hours as Mount Stewart) beyond. In 1765 Lord Bangor had one frontage designed to classical style, while m'lady insisted the other be Gothic. To the north, up the Lough's western shore, past boatyards and between fuchsia and gorse hedges, are first **Killyleagh**'s turreted fairytale castle; then crumbling Sketrick Castle; and finally the 12th-century monastic ruins of ★★ **Nendrum** (ruins all hours; visitor centre April to September, Tuesday to Saturday 10am–7pm, Sunday 2–7pm; October to March, Saturday 10am–4pm, Sunday 2–4pm); and **Castle Espie Wildlife and Wetlands Trust** reserve (summer Monday to Saturday 10.30am–5pm, Sunday 11.30am–6pm; winter Saturday 11.30am–4pm, Sunday 11.30am–5pm).

*Abbey ruins at Greyabbey*

*Mount Stewart*

# Excursion 2

## St Patrick's Country

South of Belfast on the A7 at **Saintfield**, the National Trust's **★★ Rowallane Gardens** (April to November, Monday to Friday 10.30am–6pm, weekends 2–6pm; November to March, Monday to Saturday 10.30am–5pm) are rich in rhododendron blooms each spring and hold the national collection of penstemons. The fetching Main Street includes a **Museum of Childhood** (Tuesday to Saturday 11–5pm).

Continue down the A7 to **Downpatrick**, whose name is a marriage of Patrick, this island's patron saint and apostle, and the Irish for fort (*dún*). The son of a Roman official in Wales, Patrick sailed up Stangford Lough and the Quoile to Saul where he built his first church. Patrick's

*Bucolic Rowallane Gardens*

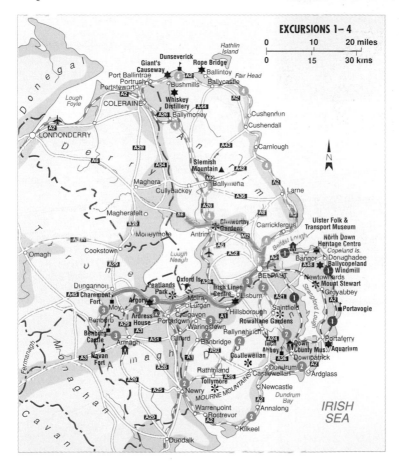

EXCURSIONS 1– 4

| 0 | 10 | 20 miles |
| 0 | 15 | 30 kms |

remains may lie under the ★ **gravestone** marked with his name at Downpatrick's Protestant ★★ **Cathedral Church of the Holy and Undivided Trinity**, or they may lie under the church itself. On the saint's day, 17 March, Downpatrick is *en fête*. A ★ **procession** wends its way from **Saul**, with its replica 10th-century round tower and tiny Protestant church, to an open-air Roman Catholic mass on a hillside beneath a towering **statue** to the saintly one. Others picnic 3km (1¼ miles) east by the healing waters of the bath-houses at Struell's ★ **St Patrick's Wells**. Still others, a mile northwest, contemplate by the Quoile in the shadow of the 1180 Cistercian ★★ **Inch Abbey** ruins.

*St Patrick's Wells at Struell*

Further attractions in Downpatrick itself include the ★ **Down County Museum** (June to August, Monday to Friday 11am–5pm, weekend 2–5pm; rest of year Tuesday to Friday 11–5pm, Saturday 2–5pm) in the 1789 gaol-house, complete with cells.

Southeast of Downpatrick, **Ardglass**'s herring port is proud of its marina and **seven castles**. Yawls from picturesque **Killough**, just to the south, once traded brandy from Bordeaux and timber from Trondheim. Along the coast past Clough's Norman motte-and-bailey ruin, sleepy **Dundrum** has a 12th-century ★★ **Norman castle** (April to September, Tuesday to Saturday 10am–7pm, Sunday 2–7pm), one of Ireland's finest.

**56**

*The Mountains of Mourne*

Then comes the Victorian resort of **Newcastle** where the compact but steep ★★★ **Mountains of Mourne** do, as the Percy French ballad describes, 'run down to the sea'. Here, the Royal County Down links is rated in the world's top 20. The range peaks at Slieve Donard's 852m (2,796ft) and is relieved by the ★ **Castlewellan** and ★ **Tollymore** Forest Parks.

The B27, which runs north from **Kilkeel**, affords fine views of the Mournes before continuing to Belfast through **Banbridge**, with its polar bear memorial to Captain Crozier, discoverer of the North West Passage, and its **Brontë Trail** commemorating local schoolmaster, Patrick, the novelists' father. Closer to the city, just off the A1, ★ **Hillsborough**, packed with antique shops and English-style pubs, is rich in Georgian architecture. **Lisburn** has its informative **Museum** and ★★★ **Irish Linen Centre** (Monday to Saturday 9.30am–5pm).

*Inside the Irish Linen Centre*

An alternative route loops south of the Mournes, west along the coast from Kilkeel past formidable 13th-century **Greencastle**. It takes in bosky ★ **Rostrevor** with its obelisk to the English Major-General Robert Ross who stormed the White House in 1814, scoffing President Madison's abandoned dinner. Beyond is breezy **Warrenpoint** with ferry to Omeath in the Republic. **Narrow Water Castle**, built in 1560, has a gruesome murder hole (July to September 11am–4.30pm, closed Wednesday).

# Excursion 3

## A Georgian flowery vale

The patron saint has two cathedrals, Catholic and Protestant, in Georgian ★★★ **Armagh**, the province's third city deep in the apple orchard county (from Belfast straight down the M1). The city's best features surround the tree-ringed sward of the ★★ **Mall**. From the Georgian terraces along the east side, burghers watched miscreants paraded from classical **courthouse** to forbidding **gaol**. The courthouse, like much in Armagh, was designed by Francis Johnston, who also gave Dublin its best houses. The ★ **County Museum** is worth a visit, as is the **Sovereign's House** with its Museum of the Royal Irish Fusiliers.

*Georgian Armagh: the Mall*

The 1790 **observatory**, to which a ★ **planetarium** was added in 1968, was built by Archbishop Robinson and Johnston. These lie off the Mall's north end near the **Royal School**, rebuilt by Robinson in 1774. Past the **Franciscan friary** ruins is Archbishop Robinson's Palace; its chapel is part of the ★ **Palace Stables Heritage Centre** where actors present prettified pasts (April to August, Monday to Saturday 10am–5.30pm, Sunday 1–6pm; September to March, Monday to Saturday 10am–5pm, Sunday 1–6pm).

*The County Museum*

**St Patrick's Trian** Visitor Centre (Monday to Saturday 10am–5pm, Sunday 2–5pm; July and August to 5.30pm) explains local links with the saint and **Jonathan Swift's** *Gulliver's Travels*, written in Gosford Castle.

The Catholic cathedral's ★★ **interior** is stunning. Not so the **exterior** of the Protestant cathedral, but here a stone marks the burial place of Brian Ború, High King of Ireland. A grotesque in the **crypt** is said to be of Patrick; another of Macha, the bare-breasted warrior queen from whom the city (Ard Macha, or Macha's Hill) takes its name. The high-tech ★★★ **Navan Centre** (April to June and September, Monday to Saturday 10am–6pm, Sunday 11am–6pm; October to March Monday to Friday 10am–5pm, Saturday 11am–5pm, Sunday noon–5pm) outside the city takes its name from a corruption of *eamhain*, the Irish for twins, after Macha's twin children.

In the surrounding countryside, best with May's apple blossom, are the pretty villages of **Moy** with its 1602 **Charlemont Fort**; **Benburb** with its chasm-edge 1615 ★ **castle**; **Loughgall** with **Dan Winter's Home** exploring the origins of the Orange Order; **Richill** with its 1664 planters' mansion; plus the linen centres of **Gilford** and **Waringstown**. Also worthy of inspection are the National Trust's two adjacent properties, the 1820 acetylene gas-lit ★★ **The Argory** and elegant ★★ **Ardress House** with its 1770s plasterwork (winter weekends and bank holidays, summer daily except Tuesday 2–6pm).

*Benburb castle*

*The Giant's Causeway*

## Excursion 4

### In the steps of a giant

*Fishing at Clotworthy Gardens*

The ★★★ **Giant's Causeway** is the province's single World Heritage Site. An astonishing sculptural composition of 40,000 huge and precisely hexagonal basalt columns, it was created when hot lava crystallised in the cold sea. Much better fun to pretend that gigantic Finn Mc-Coul began it as stepping stones to engage in fisticuffs with his Scots rival. But Finn's wife, having second thoughts, wrapped him in voluminous swaddling clothes, so when the Scot saw the size of the 'infant' he calculated the size of the father – and retreated. When Finn scooped up a sod to turf after him, it became the Isle of Man, with the hollow, Lough Neagh, the largest lake in these islands.

The approach is directly north via the M2 then the A26, with an optional diversion east to the town of **Antrim** for its Lough Neagh summer cruises, its 10th-century round tower and its ★ **Clotworthy Gardens** (open daylight hours) laid out by André Le Nôtre who created those at Versailles for Louis XIV. **Patterson's Spade Mill** (April, May and September, weekends and bank holidays; June to September daily except Tuesday 2–6pm), still water-powered though manufacture of spades ceased in 1990, is nearby.

Another diversion west could be to **Cullybackey** and the ancestral ★ **homestead**, at Dreen, of Chester Alan Arthur – one of a dozen plus US presidents, including Bill Clinton, whose ancestors were Ulster-Scots Presbyterians. To the east rises the volcanic plug of **Slemish** mountain, where St Patrick laboured as a shepherd's boy.

**Coleraine** has its **Riverside Theatre**, then come the resorts of muted **Portstewart** and brassy run-down **Portrush**, famed for its Royal Portrush Golf Links. The direct journey taking around 1½ hours. But some extra time should certainly be allowed for the turreted 14th-century ★★ **Dunluce Castle** (April to October, Monday to Saturday 10am–7pm, Sunday 2–7pm; November to March Monday to Saturday 10am–4pm, Sunday 2–4pm) below which the Spanish Armada galleas *Girona* foundered with 1,300 souls. Its artefacts rest in the Ulster Museum (*see page 28*); the rest went to the castle's chieftain, Sorley (meaning yellow-haired) Boy MacDonnel, Ireland's Rob Roy.

Time too should be left for tiny **Portballintrae** and for a tour and a dram at ★★ **Bushmills**, the oldest licensed (1609) whiskey distillery in the world. Licences to fish the Bush, a fine salmon river, can be obtained in the village.

*Tasting session at Bushmills*

To the east of the Giant's Causeway, past cliffs and white surfers' beaches, are the castle ruins at **Dunseverick** and Kinbane, plus the tiny pretty ports of **Portbraddan** and **Ballintoy**. Dunseverick, pillaged by Vikings, the capital of the ancient kingdom of Dal Riada, is one of the three great royal *dúns* (forts) of Ireland visited by St Patrick. The 20-m (65-ft) wide ★★ **Carrick-a-Rede** rope bridge swings 24m (80ft) above the waves, allowing salmon fishers and brave tourists access to a rocky promontory.

From hilly **Ballycastle** with its Folk Museum, Franciscan Friary ruins and Aul' Lammas Fair (last Monday and Tuesday in August) a ferry crosses swelling seas to ★★ **Rathlin Island** with its 100 souls outnumbered a thousand times by sea birds wheeling over its perilous cliffs (where divers quarter the many seabed wrecks) and wildflower meadows. It was while in exile on Rathlin in 1306 that Robert the Bruce took courage from a persistent spider scaling his cave's dripping walls, returning to wrest Scotland from others' hands. Should the weather grow foul, there is a pub, and a number of simple beds. But for the mythical children of Lir there was little rest: turned to swans by their jealous stepmother, they swam the Sea of Moyle between Ballycastle and Rathlin, for aeons until the ringing of St Patrick's bell brought them a merciful, and human, death.

The drive south, past **Fair Head** and following the ★★★ **Antrim Coast Road** is amongst Ireland's loveliest as the way passes the mouths, in turn, of each of the nine green glens of Antrim, moist cleavages 'tween so many hills. **Cushendun**, **Cushendall** and **Glenarm** are diverting port resorts. Carnlough's **Londonderry Arms** provides comforting delights, and at **Carrickfergus**, on Belfast Lough, stands Ireland's finest ★★ **Norman castle** (April to September, Monday to Saturday 10am–6pm, Sunday 2–6pm; October to March Monday to Saturday 10am–4pm, Sunday 2–4pm), a witness to battles lost against both the French and American navies.

59

*Aul' Lammas Fair at Ballycastle*

*The Antrim Coast*

# Architectural Heritage

*Opposite: the Marks & Spencer building*

## Lanyon's City

His insane wife committed, the novelist William Make-peace Thackeray came to Ireland, full of pathos, characterising Belfast in his 1843 *Irish Sketch-Book* as 'hearty, thriving and prosperous, as if it had money in its pockets and roast beef for dinner'. Another Englishman had arrived a few years earlier and already had his feet tucked under those moneyed tables. He was Charles Lanyon, architect, carpet-bagger and engineer. He came to Belfast from a then less prosperous Dublin, where he gained preference by marrying the boss's daughter, and was to change the city's architectural language for ever.

*Northern Bank*

He put his signature to the Antrim Coast Road, to railway viaducts and to The Frosses, avenues of firs planted to secure the bog roads. Designing Georgian country houses gained access to the milieu he sought. Soon he gave the city its originally chaste Queen's Bridge. He lent the Waring Street Belfast (now Northern) Bank and the Queen's Square Northern (now First Trust) the majestic solidity of northern Italian merchant princes' *palazzi*. His School for the Deaf and Dumb, since demolished, encouraged pride among its benefactors, humility in those who received its gruel. His drawings were truly elegant. He understood the essence of the architectural faddishness. He caught the spirit of early Victorian righteousness.

**61**

His Piranesian Crumlin Road County Gaol promises unbridled retribution. The County Courthouse's Corinthian exterior impresses with its lofty indifference, its courtrooms with academic disdain. Queen's University's spoof Elisabethanry appropriates unashamedly Oxford's Magdalen. His Doric facade of the Union Theological College promises dour Presbyterianism. His Palladian Custom House intimidates. And among his 14 churches, the campanile of Sinclair Seamen's stands as a beacon for night-time sailors. His warehouse at No. 9 Bedford Street praises naught but wealth.

*Custom House pediment*
*Sinclair Seamen's Church*

But success did not spring unsullied from the drawing board, for while Lanyon was knighted, became the city's mayor and one of its Conservative MPs, he was tainted with scandal. He was a known philanderer, and openly bought election votes. An unscrupulous property speculator, he shamelessly rigged public architectural competitions to his favour, and to the disadvantage of his great rival, W. J. Barre. However, Barre had the last laugh. A public outcry forced the City to accept a committee decision that it had sought to reverse, to award Barre, not Lanyon, the contract to design a memorial to Queen Victoria's Consort, Prince Albert. This, to a man so conscious of status, would have been his career's apogee.

## Art as History, Art as Mural

### White Horse on the Wall

HISTORY IS WRITTEN BY THE WINNER

*Republican mural*

*Red Hand of the UFF*

*1916 lily icon*

The sectarian divide between Protestant and Catholic has long been an artistic preoccupation in Belfast. A century after the victory of Protestant William of Orange over his Catholic father-in-law James II at the 1690 Battle of the Boyne, artisan coach painters celebrated with gable-end paintings of 'King Billy' riding triumphant on his white horse. When partition in 1920 hived off Northern Ireland, triumphalist Orange murals were encouraged, deflecting poor Protestants from chronic unemployment and miserable housing. It was as if the minor squirarchy that ran the Unionist Party had taken to parodying Marie Antoinette, crying 'let them paint walls'.

Until the 1981 IRA hunger strike, Nationalists and Republicans confined their icons inside political and sporting clubs. Then, with a growing confidence that they would triumph over Protestants as Protestants had over them, Republican murals were born.

Protestant murals, on the other hand, had been restricted to references to 1920s gun running, portraits of English Royals, biblical prophesies interpreted to their tradition, and portraits of William. Now Protestant paramilitaries saw their role as defenders of the faith. Contemporary military hardware appeared.

Along Sandy Row, the Shankill and the Newtownards Road, working-class Protestant heartlands, there are murals for the UDA (Ulster Defence Association ), UDF (Ulster Defence Force), UVF (Ulster Volunteer Force), UFF (Ulster Freedom Fighters), LPA (Loyalist Prisoners Association), UYM (Ulster Young Militants) and RHC (Red Hand Commando).

The UDA's murals hark back to the B-Specials (a loyalist paramilitary police force disbanded in 1969) and to Cuchulainn, Hound of Ulster, leader of the 100BC Red Branch Knights. He secured Ulster when he beat Scotland in a race to the shore by tossing his amputated hand ahead of him. Thus the Red Hand of Ulster, clenched, became the icon of LPA and UYM. The UFF added balaclava-clad men, carrying Armalite rifles. Such murals can be read at their fiercest in the light of Orange '*bonefires*' (sic) flickering on 11 July, '*Bonefire Night*'.

Meanwhile, in Catholic north and west Belfast the icons became the lily of the 1916 Easter Rising, Cuchulainn (on the Republican side), dead hunger strikers and expressions of solidarity with Mexican and Basque revolutionaries. Some read '*saoirse*' (freedom) and '*tiofaidh ár lá*', pronounced 'chucky arr lah' ('our day will come'). Others display a mordant wit in altered traffic signs: 'sniper at work', or a policeman against a no-entry red diagonal.

*Queen's University*

---

# Literary Lives

*Queen's University*

When Samuel Beckett complained of the pupils he taught at Belfast's prestigious Campbell College, his headmaster asked whether he was aware that they were the cream of Ulster society. 'Yes, rich,' Beckett replied, 'and thick.'

Luckily, few writers have been so disparaging and the city no longer automatically doffs its literary cap to its sister capital south of the border. True, Swift but lusted for Jane Waring of Waring Street. True, Oscar Wilde did little but be educated at Portora, 160km (100 miles) west, and praise the city's architecture. True, James Joyce's connection is limited to questions he put in Paris to Maurice James Craig, inspiring Craig's poem *May the Lord in His Mercy Look Down on Belfast*. But the 1947 Education Act enabled many to send the first ever of their name to university. Thus many of the greatest poets writing today in the English language cite Belfast as their catalyst. Indeed, round the Queen's University campus, there are the makings of a resonating literary trail, awaiting an entrepreneur.

The Nobel Laureate Seamus Heaney lived in Ashley Avenue and held workshops in a previous flat in Fitzwilliam Street. Many poets who passed through those critical sessions cite somewhere within a mile or so as their proving ground. Michael Longley writes of the Lisburn Road. Derek Mahon drank in Lavery's Gin Palace. Tom Paulin grew up in Belfast. James Simmons edited *The Honest Ulsterman* magazine from Eglantine Avenue. Paul Muldoon was a Queen's man. Frank Ormsby immortalised King William Park, Ciarán Carson The Fly bar, Padaic Fiacc the Holy Land east of the campus where playwrights Bill Morrison and Stewart Parker shared a flat, later rented by the novelist Maurice Leitch. Philip Larkin was assistant librarian at Queen's. The novelist and short-story writer Bernard McLaverty graduated from Queen's in

*Seamus Heaney*

63

1974, his stories throwing light on the repressed Catholic sexualities of the early 1960s.

Of an earlier generation, the prickly Ulster-Scots poet John Hewitt and E. M. Forster's friend, the novelist Forrest Reid, lived in Mount Charles. Part of poet Louis MacNeice's childhood was spent in 77 Malone Road, a bishop's palace, now the Arts Council of NI's headquarters. On his returns to Belfast he was to be found talking of rugby in Lavery's Gin Palace and the old Elbow Room. C. S. Lewis was educated at Campbell College. The poet Robert Greacen, born in 1920, went to Methodist College opposite Queen's. The novelist Brian Moore (1921–99) spent his childhood in the shadow of King Billy's equestrian statue on Clifton Street, but he wrote perceptively of the suffocating narrow conventions and sexual repressions that wrought such gloom and distress among his class-conscious priest-ridden contemporaries in fine novels, including *The Lonely Passion of Judith Hearne*.

*Mount Charles*

*Brian Moore*

The short story writer Sam McAughtry mined a different seam, reinventing the narrow red-brick streets of his impoverished Protestant childhood. Robert Harbinson, born in 1928 as Robert Harbinson Bryans in evangelical working-class east Belfast, reworked his life as cabin-boy, missionary and minor London literary lion in a series of autobiographical novels. John Boyd, a socialist from a not dissimilar background, put on his polemical plays at the Lyric Theatre while he was its literary manager.

Of other similarly lesser-known Belfast voices, worth exploring are the novels of Michael McLaverty (1904–92), particularly his *Call My Brother Back,* set at time of the Anglo-Irish War. Sam Hanna Bell, another Elbow Room regular, encouraged shipyard playwright Sam Thompson to take up his socialist pen in *Over The Bridge*. Bell's first novel, the sombre, compelling *December Bride*, explored tortured sensuality among Dissenter fishermen. Thomas Carnduff's socialist plays throw light on the roots of the troubles, as do Martin Lynch's, while the 60-plus comic volumes of George Birmingham (a.k.a. J. O. Hannay, 1865–1950) may be read as little more than curiosities, no rivals to Freeman Wills Croft's 30 crime novels.

Recent terrorism has led to many careers in confessional publishing, but of today's prose writers most pertinent are the novelists Glenn Patterson and Robert McLiam Wilson who grew up in the east and west of the city. Colin Bateman's manic thriller *Divorcing Jack* catches the black surrealism necessary for the survival of liberal consciousness. Graham Reid's television scripts and Gary Mitchell's plays, particularly *In a Little World of Our Own* and *As the Beast Sleeps*, open a window on to loyalist violence, while Ronan Bennet's fine screenplays reveal a more romantic perspective on the IRA.

# Festivals and Frolics

**Early January**: end of Christmas pantos at Grand Opera House, Waterfront Hall and Arts and Lyric Theatres.

**Early February**: Grand Opera House's opera season.

**17 March**: St Patrick's Day street parade for Ireland's national saint.

**Early April**: Between the Lines literary festival at the Crescent Arts Centre.

**Mid-May**: the province's premier agricultural show at King's Hall.

**Early June**: Holywood pub Jazz Festival, 16 km (10 miles) east of Belfast.

**June**: Belfast Civic Festival with street parades and more. Barrow Square hosts the Clarendon Dock World Music Festival, four alfresco and pub-based weekends of delight at Pat's and Rotterdam Bars. Plus late-June's Moving On Jazz Fest at the Crescent Arts Centre.

**Mid-June**: Castleward Opera season, Ireland's petite Glyndebourne (toffs 'n' tails, posh frocks 'n' opera jocks on whispering summer lawns, 50km/30 miles southeast of the city).

**Early July**: Check out if the game should be registered as an extreme sport at the Ulster Senior Hurling Finals, Casement Park.

**11 July**: Bonefire Night

**12 July**: the 'Twelfth' Orangemen's (and Women's) colourful banner-waving, bowler-hatted parades led by marching bands. Around 100,000 march in what could be the province's biggest ethno-musical tourist attraction -- if everyone loosened up.

**Mid-July**: City of Belfast International Rose Trials at Dixon Park.

**Late July**: Belfast Folk Festival

**Early August**: Féile an Phobail, the People's Festival, a celebration of Republican culture, with a pan-Celtic serious drama input, in west Belfast.

**15 August**: west Belfast's Ancient Order of Hibernians parade, akin to the Orangemen's Twelfth, only smaller

**Late August**: Ulster Grand Prix, the on-road motorcycle classic, at Dundrod, near International Airport.

**Mid-September**: Opera Northern Ireland's autumn season, Grand Opera House.

**31 October**: Hallowe'en ghosts and ghouls at various Laganside venues.

**Mid-November**: Belfast Festival at Queen's, the province's finest, a three-week gourmandising of concert, gig, drama and exhibition taking on something of the spirit of the Edinburgh Festival.

**Early December**: Cinemagic International Film Festival for the Young.

*St Patrick's Day*

*Barrow Square*

*Féile an Phobail*

# Drink and Food

## Drinking

The *Concise Ulster Dictionary* says *crack* (drink, badinage, music) derives from the Ulster Scots tongue, not the Gaelic *craic* as you might expect. While new mega-pubs (Benedict's, Franklin Gate, The Fly, Hunter's) deliver such high-decibel music you can't hear anyone speak, there are still pubs where the dominant colours are the black and creamy collar of stout (or cappuccino in café-bars), and the dominant sounds the susurration of good crack/*craic*.

The gas-lit **Crown Liquor Saloon**, on Great Victoria Street, is a symphony in tile and mirror where stage-door Johnnies proposition chorus girls in snugs. Above it is **Flannigan's**, to its right the **Beaten Docket**, named after a losing betting slip. To the left, past Emma, a ghostly chambermaid from a defunct Temperance Hotel, is **Robinson's** rebuilt façade and **Fibber Magee's**, replicating a spirit grocer's. The **Spinner's** on Blackstaff Square mines a similar Irish Disneyland.

**Morrison's Spirit Grocer's** is a more Proustian recollection with live entertainment at night. On Chichester Street the **Garrick**'s clients, once vaudevillians, are now lawyers. The **Kitchen Bar** on Victoria Square and **Bittles'** have real drinkers, with music real as their beef dinners. Skipper Street's **Crow's Nest**, hetero by day, gay by night, compliments Dunbar Street's **Parliament**, gay full-time.

In the **Mermaid** down Wilson's Court, men discuss beaten dockets. The **Morning Star** in Pottinger's Entry, one of the city's most sociable, has an oyster-house upstairs. Tiny **Benny's Bar** (a.k.a. **the A1**) on Waring Street hosts journalists reminiscing about the 1960s when Sinn Féin's Gerry Adams was barkeeper in the **Duke of York**, with its newspaper memorabilia, in Commercial Court.

Henry Joy McCracken, hero of the 1798 rebellion, hid in louche **Kelly's Cellars** in Bank Street, and jolly **White's Tavern**, down Winecellar Entry, dates from 100 years before that. In **Madden's**, in Berry Street, you'll find folk who can play bodhràn, fiddle, accordion and uillean pipes.

**Lavery's Gin Palace** mixes town and gown, while further out on Lockview Road **Cutters' Wharf** offers alfresco drinking with bulky oarsmen.

Even designers gasp at **The Fly**'s interior, a contrast to its restrained Lower Crescent Georgian facade. **Thompson's Garage** in Patterson's Lane is a far cry from all this: café-bar by day, cosmopolitan club by night, low on cleavage by provincial city club ratings. As is the cappuccino culture **Chelsea** on Lisburn Road. And if you want to hang out post-clubbing till dawn there's only one place to be: DJ David Holmes's **Mogwai** on University Road, sipping a purely medicinal Caffè Mogwai.

*The Morning Star*

*Cutter's Wharf*

*Eating out*

*The Roscoff*

## Dining

The true Belfast dish is the Ulster fry. Platters of oysters and Guinness are as rare as the leprechauns who, presumably, serve them for tourist-brochure photographs. Nevertheless, food revolutions sweep the city. First, cool chic, led by television celebrities Jeanne and Paul Rankin. Second, custom sandwich-bars. Third, the post 'peacefire' explosion of Californian-Italian bistros and American diners. Otherwise, ethnic eateries or pub champ (boiled potato mashed with butter, chives and pepper), Irish stew, or the proverbial Guinness 'n' oysters are the answer. The Lisburn Road has 50 eating houses in 2 miles.

## Restaurant selection

Listings are in three categories: **£££** = expensive (over £50 for two); **££** = moderate (£30–50 for two); **£** = inexpensive (under £30 for two).

### £££

**Roscoff**, Lesley House, Shaftesbury Square, tel: 9033 1532. Flagship of the new Belfast cuisine with chrome chairs and buttermilk walls. Try a starter of potato pancake with smoked wild salmon, chives and crème fraîche.
**Deane's**, 38–40 Howard Street, tel: 9033 1134. Young local wild pigeon, served as squab, are a strong point.
**Shanks**, Blackwood Golf Centre, Crawfordsburn Road, Bangor, tel: 028-9185 3313. Roscoff's only rival, 19 km (12 miles) northeast of Belfast.

### ££

**Aerø**, 44 Bedford Street, tel: 9024 4844. Balsamic, pangrilled and tapanade are the key words here.
**Alto's**, 6 Fountain Lane, tel: 9032 3087. Celtic music-buff Éamonn O'Catháin tosses exotic oil salads in Californian-Italian style.
**Antica Roma**, 67 Botanic Avenue, tel: 9031 1121. *Trompe l'oeil* Roman villa with Little Italy baby grand, bringing Latin flair to Irish seafood.

*Café Society*

**Archana**, 53 Dublin Road, tel: 9032 3717. Best balti.
**(La) Belle Époque**, 61 Dublin Road, tel: 9032 3244. Beef, brill and pigeon in the best bourgeois tradition.
**Café Society**, 3 Donegall Square West, tel: 9042 9525. With the best people-watching city-centre window, a bistro Mediterannean menu.
**Chez Delbart**, 10 Bradbury Place, tel: 9023 8020. So packed it won't take bookings. One of a quartet founded by a Breton, Jean Delbart. Called Frogities by habitués.
**Jharna Tandoori**, 133 Lisburn Road, tel: 9038 1299. 'Jewel in the Crown' decor matches Bangladeshi enthusiasm.
**Láziz**, 99 Botanic Avenue, tel: 9023 4888. Moroccan specialities including cous cous.

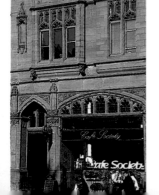

**Manor House**, 47 Donegall Pass, tel: 9023 8755. Lough Neagh eels from Europe's largest fishery are listed amongst the swallow's nest soups.

*Crown Liquor Saloon*

**Nick's Warehouse**, 35 Hill Street, tel: 9043 9690. Nick Price's trio – wine bar, café, then serious restaurant – serve terrific lunchtime salads and casseroles whilst upstairs diners tuck into duck, get hearty over halibut.

**Opus One**, 1 University Street, tel: 9059 0606. Bistro chic.

**Rajput**, 461 Lisburn Road, tel: 9066 2168. Friendly north Indian.

**Ruby Tuesday's**, 629A Lisburn Road, tel: 9066 1220 & 157 Stranmillis Road, tel: 9066 7749. 'Ruby' specialises in read-the-papers Ulster Fry breakfasts.

*Breads for breakfast*

**(La) Salsa**, 21 University Road, tel: 9024 4588. Margaritas by the litre wash down South-of-the (other) Border fare midst abobe colours.

**Summer Palace**, 126 Great Victoria Street, tel: 9023 5828. The city's Chinese are amongst the louche in this late-hours establishment.

**Sun Kee**, 38 Donegall Pass, tel: 9031 2016. The excellence of this restaurant's Chinese dishes entirely justifies recent price increases.

**Tedford's Fish Restaurant**, 5 Donegall Quay, tel: 9043 4000. Delicious fresh fish.

**Villa Italia**, 39 University Road, tel: 9032 8356. Everybody queues for popular pastas.

**£**

**Bishop's**, 32 Bradbury Place, tel: 9031 1827. Replica of the quality fish 'n' chipper. Ceramic tiles, mushy peas, pots of tea and an open (gas) fire.

**Doorsteps**, 455 Lisburn Road, tel: 9068 1645. Big tasty sandwiches.

**Long's Fish Restaurant**, 39 Athol Street, tel: 9032 1848. An old fashioned chippy. A Belfast institution.

## Pub grub

Recommended for honest fare: **Crown Liquor Saloon**, 46 Great Victoria Street, tel: 9024 9476, **Morning Star**, 17 Pottinger's Entry, tel: 9032 3976, the **Kitchen Bar**, 16 Victoria Square, tel: 9032 4901, **Bittles' Bar**, 70 Upper Church Lane, tel: 9031 1088, **Garrick**, 29 Chichester Street, tel: 9033 3875, **Magennis's Whiskey Café**, 83 May Street, tel: 9023 0295, **McHugh's**, 29–31 Queen's Square, tel: 9024 7830. **Morrison's Spirit Grocers**, 21 Bedford Street, tel: 9024 8458, and **Lavery's Gin Palace**, 12 Bradbury Place, tel: 9032 7159.

*A booming club scene*

## Late night

The bar/club scene is booming in Belfast. Fashions change, but constants on the club beat include:

**Madison's**, Botanic Avenue, tel: 9033 0040. Chart music, no jeans.

**M-Club**, Bradbury Place, tel: 9023 3131. Commercial dance, a provincial obsession with B-list celebrities and vertiginous cleavages.

**Paradise Lost** (Europa Hotel), 25 Glengall Street, tel: 9026 6060. Easy listening, brassy.

**Shine**, Students Union, University Road. Techno tastes, schoolgirl chic.

**Storm** (a.k.a. Bob's), Lisburn Road, tel: 9033 2526. Chart music, no sports wear.

**Thompson's Garage**, Patterson's Place, tel: 9032 3762. House and garage music with a glam or scam dress code.

**Parliament**, 2 Dunbar Street, tel: 9023 4520. Gay.

**Crow's Nest**, Skipper Street, tel: 9027 9924. Gay.

**Duke of York**, 11 Commercial Court, tel: 9024 1062. Lesbian on Thursdays.

## Jazz

**Belfast Boat Club**, Lockview Road, tel: 9066 5012.

**Cutter's Wharf**, Lockview Road, tel: 9066 2501. Sunday jazz brunch.

**White's Tavern**, 2–12 Winecellar Entry, tel: 9024 3080. Thursdays.

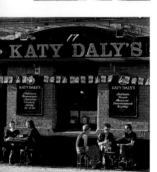

*Katy Daly's*

**Katy Daly's**, 17 Ormeau Road, tel: 9032 5942. Home to the city's singer-songwriters.

**Larry's Wine Bar**, 36 Bedford Street, tel: 9032 5061. A wine-fuelled knees-up.

## Traditional music

Irish traditional music crosses the sectarian divide:

**Madden's**, 74 Smithfield, tel: 9024 4144. The real McCoy.

**Kitchen Bar**, 16 Victoria Square, tel: 9032 4901. Also authentic playing.

Less purist are **The Empire**, Botanic Avenue, tel: 9032 8110, and **Kelly's Cellars**, 30 Bank Street, tel: 9032 4835.

# Shopping

*Castlecourt Shopping Mall*

Once local stores lined routes to City Hall. Now up Donegall Place and Royal Avenue you run the gamut of British chain stores from Argos to Waterstone's. But from the top of Castlecourt shopping mall's car park – with car or not – there's the best **view of the city**, a 360-degree panorama. There are other visual benefits: **Tesco**, Royal Avenue, once the Provincial Bank of Ireland with its 1869 façade of kings' heads, has a marvellously airy domed interior.

Once tributary lanes and workaday roads were rich in boot and cycle-repair shops, haberdashers, newsagents. Now these are given over to cafés and mobile-phone rental, though the Lisburn Road still feels like the 'real' Belfast.

Specialists still trade. **Alexander the Grate** is notable among Donegall Pass's architectural-salvage arcades. **Back in Time**, a deconsecrated Antrim Road church, is a cornucopia of antique ephemera from anchor to xylophone, with nearby **Emerald Books** a bibliophile's dusty dream. **Smyth's Irish Linens** in Royal Avenue sells time-warp souvenirs. Bedford Street's **Craftworks** markets local potters and weavers, while nearby **Steenson's** has more original, if expensive, Ulster-designed silver and gold. **Equinox** in Howard Street specialises in glass and tableware. **Good Vibrations,** along the street, is the most eclectic of record shops.

*Marcus Music Shop on Royal Avenue*

For clothes, Irish designer **Paul Costelloe** in Bradbury Place is a must-see. For food, the **Arcadia** and **Cargoes** on Lisburn Road are praised delicatessens, and **St George's Market** and Fountain Lane's **Sawers** have good Irish cheese and fish. **Direct Wine Shippers** in Corporation Square has a fine selection of wines, Irish whiskeys and Scotch. And for the footsore **McKernan's** in North Street Arcade has been cobbling bespoke boots for minor royals since time (almost) immemorial.

# Getting There

*Opposite: the Campbeltown–Ballycastle ferry*

## By Air

Belfast International (tel: 028-94484848), 30km (19 miles) northwest of the city, is Northern Ireland's busiest airport with connections from the rest of the UK, Europe and US. The smaller Belfast City Airport (tel: 028-9045 7745) is 4 miles (6km) from the city centre.

Numerous daily services link Belfast International with Heathrow or Stansted (one hour) and eight UK airports. British Airways (tel: 0345-222111) and British Midland (tel: 0845-6071630) offer frequent London connections. EasyJet (tel: 0870-6000000) caters for budget travellers ex-Luton. Sabena (tel: 020-8780 1444) flies from Brussels and Air UK/KLM (tel: 0990-074074) from Amsterdam. British Midland's Paris services touch down at East Midlands en-route. Aer Lingus (tel: 0645-737747) has four weekly services from New York via Shannon. Charter operators such as American Trans Air run summer services.

The City of Belfast Airport has flights from UK provincial airports, plus London's Gatwick, Luton and Stansted (Jersey European, tel: 028-9045 7200). Weekday flights link the airport with Cork (Newquay Air, tel: 00353-21316900), Derry (Jersey European), Düsseldorf (Gill Air, tel: 0191-214 6666) and Paris (BA). London airports all have rail/subway or bus connections to central London.

To get to Belfast city centre from from International Airport there is a half-hourly Airbus (tel: 028-9033 3000). City Airport has rail links to Central and Great Victoria Street Stations. Taxis are plentiful from both airports.

## By Sea

Norse Irish Ferries (tel: 0151-944 1010) offers an 11-hour car ferry from Liverpool; P&O European Ferries (tel: 0990-980980) nine 1-hour car ferries daily into Larne, 35km (22 miles) north of Belfast, from Cairnryan, Scotland; SeaCat (tel: 0345-523523) five 90-minute catamaran and StenaLine (tel: 0990-204204) nine 105-minute sailings to Stranraer-Belfast. There are two summer services: the Argyll & Antrim Steam Packet Company (tel: 0345-523523), from Campbeltown in Scotland to Ballycastle, 96km (60 miles) north of Belfast; the Isle of Man Steam Packet Company (tel: 01641-661661), from Douglas to Belfast.

*Portaferry–Strangford ferry*

## By Train & Coach

Both rail and buses run frequent Dublin/Belfast expresses. The train, run by Northern Ireland Railways (tel: 028-9089 9411) and Iarnród Éireann into Central Station is quicker but more expensive. Free buses link Great Victoria and Central Stations. Ulsterbus (tel: 028-9033 3000) also runs services from London and major British cities.

## Getting Around

### Buses and trains

Red Citybuses (tel: 028-9024 6485) radiate from City Hall, their timetables displayed at departure points and Bus-Centres. Buy single tickets from the driver, and multi-journey ones from kiosks and newsagents. Citybus operates 2–3 hour tours (tel: 028-9045 8484).

Blue single-decker Ulsterbuses (tel: 028-9033 3000) serve suburbs and province. The main depots are the Europa BusCentre and Laganside BusCentre by the Albert Clock, but they pick up and set down at hard-to-spot stops inside city limits. Freedom of Northern Ireland tickets permit unlimited bus and train travel. Ulsterbus's Irish Rover covers all of Ireland.

Northern Ireland Railways operate east to Bangor, northeast to Larne, northwest to Derry, and south to Dublin. Commuter trains from Central or Great Victoria Street Stations to Botanic provide campus area access.

*Europa BusCentre*

### Taxis

There are taxi ranks at City Hall, Crown Bar, airports and main stations. Drivers at Central station pack London-style hackneys until full for a particular direction (only the strong-willed confront this illegal practice). An alternative is to phone a 'radio cab' such as City Cab (tel: 028-9024 2000) from Botanic; Fast Taxis (tel: 028-9045 8011) from Central Station; Value Cabs (tel: 028-9023 0000) from Great Victoria Street; VIP (tel: 028-9066 6111) University area. Members of the West Belfast Taxi Drivers' Association run guided trouble-spot tours, an essential Belfast experience. Departing when full, they run into once difficult areas from Bridge Street and North Street Upper.

*Cycling on the flat*

### Driving and cycling

The city has many parking lots, and on-street pay-and-display parking is generous. Donegall Place and its tributaries are pedestrianised, but only in theory. Driving is to the left; speed limits are – with clearly signed exceptions – 30mph (50kmh) in built-up areas, 60mph (95kmh) outside built-up areas and 70mph (112kmh) on motorways. Seat belts are mandatory as are crash helmets for motorcyclists.

Cycling is a good way to see this flat city. Bikes can be hired from: McConvey Cycles (10 Pottinger's Entry, tel: 9033 0322) and ReCycle (1–5 Albert Square, tel: 9031 3113).

### Walking tours

Belfast Walks (tel: 028-9268 3665) offers, among others, a Bailey's Historical Pub Tour, run in association with the Blue Badge Northern Ireland Tour Guides Associates, tel: 028-9062 9592, e-mail: Hood@totalweb.co.uk.

# Facts for the Visitor

*St George's Market*

## Tourist Information

The Northern Ireland Tourist Board's main Information Centre is in St Anne's Court, 59 North Street, Belfast BT1 1NB, tel: 028-9024 6609, fax: 028-9024 0960, e-mail: general.enquiries.nitb@nics. gov.uk. (September to June Monday to Saturday 9.15am–5.15pm, July to August 9.15am–7pm Monday to Saturday, Sunday noon–4pm).

The walk to the office down North Street is depressing. Best to approach through the gardens of Cathedral Close on Donegall Street opposite St Anne's Cathedral. The centre also provides information via a wall-mounted touch-sensitive screen outside office hours, and credit-card accommodation booking service (tel: 0800-404050).

There are also information points at both airports.

Before you arrive, you can obtain information from the British Tourist Authority in many countries, or:
*UK*: Northern Ireland Tourist Board, 11 Berkeley Street, London W1X 5AD, tel: 020-7355 5040, fax: 020-7409 0847, freephone 0800-282662. Northern Ireland Tourist Board, 135 Buchanan Street, 1st floor, Glasgow G1 2JA, tel: 0141-204 4454, fax: 0141-204 4454. All Ireland Travel Desk, British Travel Centre, 12 Regent Street, Piccadilly Circus, London SW1(personal callers only).
*Republic of Ireland*: Northern Ireland Tourist Board, 16 Nassau Street, Dublin 2, tel: Dublin 6791977, Callsave 1850-230230, fax: 6791863.
*US*: 551 Fifth Avenue, Suite 701, New York, NY 10176, tel: (212) 922 0101 or 800-326 0036, fax: (212) 922 0099, e-mail: info@northern-ireland.com.
*Canada*: Northern Ireland Tourist Board, 111 Avenue Road, Suite 450, Toronto, Ontario M5R 3J8, tel: (416) 925 6368, fax: (416) 961 2175.

*A good vantage point on St Patrick's Day*

*Assembly Rooms clock*

*Ulster Bank*

*Australasia*: All Ireland Tourism, Level 5, 36 Carrington Street, Sydney, NSW 2000, tel: (02) 299 6177, fax: (02) 299 6323.

## Time
Belfast follows Greenwich Mean Time. In spring clocks are turned one hour forward but revert to GMT in autumn.

## Shopping Hours
City centre shops are open 9am–5.30pm Monday to Saturday, with later evening opening (till 9pm) Thursday and Saturday. Large stores open 1–4pm on Sunday. Many local shops and fuel station shops keep much longer hours.

## Banks and Currency
Banking hours are 9.30am–4.30pm, with some village branches 10.30am–3.30pm with lunchtime closing. A few larger branches open Saturday morning. 24-hour cash dispensers (ATMs) are plentiful in city centre and campus areas. Currency is the British pound sterling, but the province's banks (Bank of Ireland, First Trust, Northern and Ulster Banks) issue their own notes. Though these are also legal tender in Great Britain it is wise to change your money to Bank of England notes before leaving for the mainland. The currency of the Republic of Ireland, the pound or punt, must be exchanged at the going rate but many big stores will accept them without charging commission.

## New Telephone Numbers
A new single code, 028 (44-28 from outside the UK), accesses the whole of Northern Ireland and is used throughout this book. In addition, old five-and six-figure numbers are prefaced by two or three digits to turn them into eight-digit numbers – 90 for Belfast, 71 for Derry, 37 for Armagh, and so on. Previous codes (such as 01232 for Belfast) will not work after September 2000.

## Mail
The main post office is in Castle Place. The Tomb Street depot provides late posting.

## Emergencies
Ambulance, coastguard, fire, police: dial 999, or 112.

## Public Holidays
New Year's Day (1 January), St.Patrick's Day (17 March), Easter Monday*, May Day (1st Monday in May), Spring Bank Holiday (last Monday in May), Orangeman's Day (12 July if not a Sunday), Summer Bank Holiday (last Monday in August), Christmas Day (25 December), Boxing Day (26 December).

# Belfast for Children

*Activities at Barnett's Demesne*

There's a prehistoric dolmen in the 200-m (600-ft) diameter ringed enclosure, the **Giant's Ring**, just south of Shaw's Bridge. The city's 53 parks –particularly **Dixon Park** with its nature study area, **Lagan Valley Regional Park** with its riverside trails, **Barnett's Demense** with its walks, and **Cavehill Country Park** with its caves – provide rolling picnicking acres. Beside Cavehill is **Belfast Zoo** which has underwater viewing of sea lion and penguin, a Spider Monkey Island and Polar Bear Canyon, plus a breeding programme specialising in elephant, giraffe and zebra. Cuddlier animals are on tap at **Springvale Open Dairy Farm,** Ballyhanwood Road, with nature trail, pony and tractor rides, and animal feeding.

The **Botanical Gardens** with **Tropical Ravine** complete with banana trees and monster water lilies, plus **Palm House** (more banana trees) are more accessible. Here too is the **Ulster Museum** with Egyptian mummy, stuffed Irish wolfhound, dinosaur, Early Ireland 'discovery drawers' and interactive activities. The **People's Museum**, Shankill Road, recreates the 1930s, and **Lagan Lookout Centre** opts for hands-on computer images of the river's past and present (*see page 34*). But pride of place goes to the **Ulster Folk and Transport Museum** (*see page 53*).

*Ulster Folk and Transport Museum*

**Circus Belfast,** Crescent Arts Centre, runs tiny circus skills courses for tiny bodies. **Dundonald Ice Bowl,** 5km (3 miles) east, introduces kids to its Olympic-sized ice rink and Indiana Land adventures; while 25km (15 miles) to the south, at Crossgar, the **Ulster Wildlife Centre** offers nature close up; as does Seaforde's **Butterfly Garden** 32km (20 miles) to the south. **Dreamworld** on Boucher Road and **Planet Leisure** at Yorkgate are commercial 'family play' centres. **Maud's Ice-cream Factory** at Glenoe, past Carrickfergus, runs tasty factory visits.

## Accommodation

The Northern Ireland Tourist Board's *Where to Stay in Northern Ireland* booklet, on sale at TICs and bookshops, classifies hotels and self-catering establishments on a one to five star basis, guesthouses A to B, while B&Bs have no grading but must register with, and display the approval sign of, the NITB. For a short stay, an A class guesthouse in the south of the city could be more comfortable and conveniently located than more expensive two-star hotels.

### ££££ (over £150 double)

**Culloden Hotel**, 142 Bangor Road, tel: 9042 5223. This former bishop's palace run by the Hastings family maintains a restrained presence while permitting the *frisson* of a late dram, to be worked off the next morning in the indoor pool or fitness centre.

*Europa Hotel*

**Europa Hotel**, Great Victoria Street, tel: 9032 7000. Billy Hastings' city-centre hotel is proud of its history as western Europe's most bombed. Bill and Hillary Clinton spent a night there. Located by the Grand Opera House, it hosts divas, chorus girls and well-preserved thespians.

**Forte Posthouse**, 300 Kingsway, Dunmurry, tel: 9061 2101. Relocating to Ormeau Avenue at the end of 1999.

**Hilton Belfast**, Lanyon Place, tel: 9027 7000. Spearheading the Lagan's gentrification, this is a middle-range Hilton overlooking Waterfront Hall.

*Prize-winning breakfast*

**McCausland Hotel**, Victoria Street, tel: 9022 0200. Thomas Fitzpatrick's superb carvings (*see page 36*) decorate this elegant conversion from warehouse to hotel. Convenient for centre and 'cultural quarter'.

**Stormont Hotel**, 587 Upper Newtownards Road, tel: 9065 8621. Business hotel in the Hastings chain.

**Wellington Park Hotel**, 21 Malone Road, tel: 9038 1111. Flagship of the Mooney family empire, this expanded off-campus mansion is loved by academic and agency gurus appreciative of its singles-bar's reputation.

### £££ (over £75 double)

**L'Acadamie**, 14 College Gardens, tel: 9066 6046. Though Mrs Aubrey prefers to let her airy 4-bed self-catering apartments by the week, she will take overnight guests.

**Duke's**, 65 University Street, tel: 902 36666. Much favoured spacious corner rooms, just across from the Queen's Film Theatre above a bar beloved of academics.

**Holiday Inn Garden Court**, 15 Brunswick Place, tel: 9033 3555. Conveniently situated behind the Crown Liquor Saloon and operated by Diljit Rana, a Punjabi who has done much to revive the south city centre.

**Jurys Belfast Inn**, Fisherwick Place, tel: 9053 3500. Not, from the exterior, the city's loveliest, the view from its north facing rooms, of Sir John Soane's Royal Belfa. demical Institution, is the city's classiest.

**Madison's**, Botanic Avenue, tel: 9033 0044. Fizzy addition to the Mooney empire, this is one of a duo of refurbished designer bistro hotels.

**Renshaw's**, 75 University Street, tel: 9033 3366. Wood-floored bar full of students. Culture vultures' haunt.

**Shaftesbury Plaza**, 7–21 Bradbury Place, tel: 9024 6161. Overlooking the city's fast-food strip next door to the rent-a-minor-celebrity M-Club, the Shaftesbury's clientele are more akin to Madison's and the Townhouse's.

**The Townhouse**, 8 Lower Crescent, tel: 9023 3349. Provided Madison's with its first competition in style.

*Townhouse Hotel*

## ££ (over £50 double)

**Ash-Rowan Guest House**, 12 Windsor Avenue, tel: 9066 1758. Although near the international football pitch, this splendid Victorian affectation houses more fastidious travel writers than tabloid sports writers.

**Holiday Inn Express**, 106 University Street, tel: 9031 1909. Budget end of Holiday Inn/Rana partnership.

**Lisdara**, 23 Derryvolgie Avenue, Malone Road, tel: 9068 1549. Stylish Victorian house in leafy suburbs.

**Old Rectory**, 148 Malone Road, tel: 9066 7882. Pastel decorations complement the complimentary evening fireside whiskey served at this prestigious 1896 rectory.

**Queen's University Common Room**, 1 College Gardens, tel: 9066 5938. Functional campus rooms. Good bar.

**Stranmillis Lodge**, 14 Chlorine Gardens, tel: 9068 2009. Once allegedly a hideaway for spooks and mandarins, now an oasis of calm seclusion.

**Tara Lodge**, 36 Cromwell Road, tel: 9059 0900. A deconsecrated church which became theatrical rehearsal rooms, now entirely rebuilt.

## £ (under £40 double)

**Ark**, 18 University Street, tel: 9032 9626. Affordable.

**Arnie's Backpackers**, 63 Fitzwilliam Street, tel: 9024 2876. The name says it all. Near station. Cheap.

**Belfast International Youth Hostel**, 22 Donegall Road, tel: 9032 4733. With family rooms. Cheap.

**(The) Cottage**, 377 Comber Road, Dundonald, tel: 9087 8189. With just two rooms 8km (5 miles) east of the city centre, Mrs Muldoon's white-washed thatched roof cottage is always booked well ahead.

**232 Duncairn Gardens**, tel: 9074 5550. Currently one of the few approved guesthouses within walking distance of a 'flash-point' area.

**Young Women's Christian Association Hostel**, Queen Mary's Hall, 70 Fitzwilliam Street, tel: 9024 0439. Closed Easter and Christmas.

# Index

...ways)39–40
...asic Hall......29

...Road................50–1
...avals ......................65
...rst Presbyterian
   Church ..................44
First Trust Bank ........33
Fly, The, public house.26

...57
...57

...59
...state ......51
...................53
...Demesne 52, 77
...W.J. ................61
...ow Square ............35
...lfast Castle ......46–7
Belfast Institute ......23–4
Belfast Telegraph ......43
Belvoir Forest Park .....52
Bittles' Bar ............36, 67
Botanic Gardens ....28, 77

**C**arrickfergus ...........59
Castle Place .......44–5, 49
Castlecourt
   shopping mall ..........43
Cavehill
   Country Park ..46–7, 77
Cirque & Grand
   Opera House ............21
City Hall ............37–8, 49
Civic Arts Theatre.......29
Clarendon Dock .........35
Clifton House .......42, 51
climate .....................5–6
Clotworthy Gardens ...58
clubs ..........................70
Crawfordsburn ...........53
Crescent Arts Centre ...26
Crescent Church.........26
Crescent Gardens .......26
Crown Courthouse 43, 61
Crown Entry...............39
Crown Liquor
   Saloon ..................22–3
Crumlin Road.......43, 51
Custom House .......33, 61
Cutter's Wharf......52, 67

**D**onaghadee.............53–4
Donegall Place ...........45
Donegall Quay ...........34
Donegall Street..41–2, 49
Downpatrick ...........55–6
Dublin Road ...............20
Dundrum Castle .........56
Dunluce Castle ...........59

**G**arrick Bar ..........36, 67
Giant's Causeway ...58–9
Giant's Ring dolmen ...52
Glass Jar, The.............39
Grand Opera House
   *see Cirque*
Grand Orange Lodge
   of Ireland .................20
Great Victoria Street ..21
Greyabbey ruins .........54
Group Theatre .......17–18

**H**arland & Wolff
   shipyard ........9, 35, 50
Harland, Sir Edward
   James, statue of ........36
Harbour Office ........34–5
High Street ............40, 44
Hill Street ..................41
Hillsborough ..............56
history ..........6–8, 10–11
Holy Land ..................29

**I**nch Abbey................56
Industry ...................8–9
Irish Linen Centre ......52
Irish News ..................42

**J**oy Street .................32

**K**elly's Cellars.............45
King Billy, statue of ....43
King William Park ......26
Kitchen Bar ..........36, 67

**L**agan, river ...........34, 52
Lagan Valley Nature
   Reserve ...............52, 77
Lagan Weir and Lookout
   Centre .........34, 52, 77
Lanyon, Charles ......9, 61
Lavery's
   Gin Palace ..........25, 67
linen.......................8–9
Linen Hall House ........17
Linen Hall Library 15–16
literature .................63–4
Lyric Theatre.........28, 64

**M**adison's Hotel ...29, 79
Magennis's Whiskey
   Café & Public House 32
Marks & Spencer
   building................38, 61
Marquess of Dufferin
   and Ava, statue of.....38
Masonic Building.........39
May Street .................31
McArt's Fort ..............47
McCausland's Hotel....36
McHugh's Bar.............33
Morrison's Spirit
   Grocers ...............19–20
Mount Charles......26, 64
Mount Stewart............54
Mourne Mountains......56
murals...................48, 62

**N**endrum ruins ...........54
News Letter, former
   offices of............41, 49
Northern Bank.......40, 61
Northern Ireland
   Tourist Board...........32
Northern Ireland War
   Memorial Building ...40
North Street Arcade ....41

**O**ld Museum ..............24
Ormeau Baths Gallery.19
Ormeau Bridge......50, 52
Ormeau Embankment .52

**P**alm House ...............28
Portaferry ..................54
Pottinger's Entry ...39–40
Presbyterian Assembly
   Rooms......................23
Provincial Bank
   building....................43
pubs and bars..............67

**Q**ueen Elizabeth
   Bridge.................49–50
Queen's Bridge ...........33
Queen's Film Theatre..29
Queen's Island 35, 50, 52
Queen's Square ...........33
Queen's University .27–8

**R**athlin Island .............59
religion .......6, 48–51, 62
restaurants ...............68–9
Reverend Henry Cooke,
   statue of, ..................24
Riverside Walk......34, 52
Robinson's Bar......23, 67

Roscoff restaurant .20, 68
Rowallane Gardens .....55
Royal Belfast Acad-
   emical Institution......23
Royal Courts
   of Justice..................33

**S**t Anne's Cathedral....41
St George's Church.....36
St George's Market ....32
St Joseph's Church......35
St Malachy's
   Church ................18–19
St Patrick's Church .....42
St Paul's Church .........43
Samson & Goliath ......35
Sandy Row .................50
Scottish Provident
   Institution ................16
Shaftesbury Square20, 25
Shankill Road..............51
shopping ......................71
Short Strand ...............50
Sinclair Seamen's
   Church ................35, 61
Sir Thomas and Lady
   Dixon Park...............52
Springmartin estate .....51
Strangford Lough ........54

**T**homas Thompson
   Memorial .................19
*Titanic* ...............30–1, 35
Titanic memorial.........31
tourist information ......75
transportation .........73–4
Turf Lodge estate ........51

**U**lster Bank .......20–1, 40
Ulster Folk & Transport
   Museum ..............53, 77
Ulster Hall .................17
Ulster Museum......28, 77
Union Theological
   College ...............29, 61
University
   Conservation Area....26
University Square....26–7

**V**ictoria Street.......36, 49

**W**aterfront Hall.....32, 52
Whiterock estate..........51
White's Tavern......44, 67

**Y**orkshire House ...16–17

**Z**oo..............................47